ᵀᴴᴱREP
Birmingham Repertory Theatre

presents

hester

The World Premiere of

Behzti (Dishonour)

by Gurpreet Kaur Bhatti

First performed at Birmingham Repertory Theatre
on 9 December 2004

Birmingham Repertory Theatre
Centenary Square
Broad Street
Birmingham
B1 2EP

www.birmingham-rep.co.uk

ᵀᴴᴱREP
Birmingham Repertory Theatre

Behzti (Dishonour)
by Gurpreet Kaur Bhatti

Cast in order of appearance

Balbir	**Shelley King**
Min	**Yasmin Wilde**
Elvis	**Jimmy Akingbola**
Giani Jaswant	**Munir Khairdin**
Mr Sandhu	**Madhav Sharma**
Teetee	**Harvey Virdi**
Polly	**Pooja Kumar**

Director	**Janet Steel**
Designer	**Matthew Wright**
Lighting Designer	**Mark Doubleday**

Stage Manager	**Ali Biggs**
Assistant Stage Manager	**Olly Seviour**

Cast

Shelley King Balbir

Shelley was born in Calcutta, and trained at the Webber Douglas Academy Of Dramatic Art.
Theatre: Shelley most recently played Sylvie in *Calcutta Kosher* (Kali Theatre and Stratford East); Dr Bannerji in Tanika Gupta's adaptation of *Hobson's Choice* (Young Vic and tour); and Kitty Da Souza in *Bombay Dreams* (West End original cast). Other theatre credits include: *Behsharam* (Soho Theatre and Birmingham Repertory Theatre); *River On Fire* (Kali Theatre); *Macbeth* and *Measure For Measure* (Theatre Unlimited); *The Crutch* (Royal Court); *Orpheus*, *The Modern Husband* and *Ion* (Actors Touring Company); *A Midsummer Night's Dream*, *Troilus And Cressida*, *Heer Ranjha*, *Danton's Death* and *Antigone* (Tara Arts); *Dance Like A Man* and *Naga Mandala* (Leicester Haymarket); *Damon And Pythias* (Globe Theatre); *Top Girls* (Royal Theatre Northampton); *Women Of Troy*, *Tartuffe* and *The Little Clay Cart* (National Theatre); *Death And The Maiden* (Wolsey Theatre Ipswich); *Cloud Nine* (Manchester Contact Theatre); *The Innocent Mistress* (Derby Playhouse) and *Privates On Parade* (Edinburgh Royal Lyceum).
Television includes: *Silent Witness*, *See How They Run*, *A Secret Slave*, *Real Women*, *Where The Heart Is*, *The Demon Headmaster*, *The Bill*, *Casualty*, *Brookside*, *The Jewel In The Crown*, *King Of The Ghetto*, *Rockcliffe's Babies*, *South Of The Border* and two series of *Tandoori Nights* and *Angels*.
Film includes: Da Cruz in *Code 46*.
Radio: Shelley has made numerous recordings for BBC Radio 4.

Yasmin Wilde Min

Yasmin trained at the Webber Douglas Academy Of Dramatic Art after graduating from Cambridge University.
Theatre credits include: Alithea in *The Country Wife* (Watford Palace Theatre); Durga in *Hobson's Choice* (Young Vic); Mrs Joe/Molly in *Great Expectations* (Unicorn Theatre); The Queen in *Sleeping Beauty* (Northampton Theatre Royal); Lydia Languish in *The Rivals* and female roles in *The Blue Room* (Worcester Swan); *Arabian Nights* (Young Vic and world tour); *The Jungle Book* and *Arabian Nights* (mac); *Airport 2000*(Greenwich); *Gulliver's Travels* (London Bubble Theatre); *Shakers* (Hull Truck Theatre); *Heavenly Bodies* (Leicester Haymarket) and *The Jungle Book* (Manchester Library Theatre).
Radio credits include: Rahel in *The God Of Small Things* and Chitra in *Bhopal* (BBC Radio 4)
Television credits include: *EastEnders*, *My Hero*, *Jonathan Creek*, *The Bill*, *Teenage Health Freak* and *HTV Challenge Trial*.

Jimmy Akingbola Elvis

Jimmy trained at ALRA.
Theatre credits include: *Nativity*, *The Ramayana*, *Naked Justice* and *The Shooky* (Birmingham Repertory Theatre); *People Next Door* (Traverse/Theatre Royal Stratford East); *Playing Fields* (Soho Theatre); *Naked Justice* (West Yorkshire Playhouse); *The Ramayana* (National Theatre); *Baby Doll* (National Theatre/West End) and *Ready Or Not Raw* (Theatre Royal Stratford East).
TV credits include: *The Crouches*, *Stupid*, *Who Killed PC Blakelock?*, *Roger Roger*, *Doctors*, *Slightly Filthy Show* and *The South Bank Show*.
Radio: *The Amen Corner*, *A Noise In The Night*, *Clothes Of Nakedness*, *West Way* and *Trinidad Sisters* (BBC World Service; *Dancing Backwards* (Radio 4) and *Fire Children* (Radio 3).
Film includes: *Just Gaps* and *Anansi*.

Munir Khairdin Giani Jaswant

Theatre credits include: *Romeo And Juliet* (Changeling Theatre); *Bombay Dreams* (Apollo Victoria); *Rashomon* and *The Butcher's Skin* (Yellow Earth Theatre); *The Odyssey/The Ramayana* (Tara Arts tour); *Kafka's The Trial* (Cherub Company); *Bollywood 2000 – Yet Another Love Story* (The Reduced Indian Film Company tour); *Romeo And Juliet* (Leicester Haymarket); *The Merchant Of Venice* (Cherub Company).
Film includes: *It Was An Accident*.

Madhav Sharma Mr Sandhu

It all began with touring Shakespeare in India, Singapore, Malysia, Sarawak, Brunei, North Borneo and Hong Kong, followed by a scholarship to RADA and a career of some four decades so far.
Theatre includes; *Calcutta Kosher*, *Worlds Apart*, *House Of The Sun* (Theatre Royal Stratford East); *The King And I* (West End and tour); *The Accused* (Haymarket and tour); *Last Dance At Dum Dum* (New Ambassadors/tour); *Crazy Horse* (Bristol New Vic/tour); *Not Just An Asian Babe* (Watermans); *Indian Ink* (Aldwych); *High Diplomacy* (Westminster); *Untold Secret Of Aspi* (Cockpit); *Thérèse Raquin* (Nottingham Playhouse); *Twelfth Night* (Dundee Theatre Royal); *Romeo And Juliet* (Shaw/Edinburgh Festival/USA); *The Importance Of Being Neutral* (ICA); *Fiddler On The Roof* (tour); *Blithe Spirit* (Birmingham Repertory Theatre); and the title role in *Hamlet* (The Howff).
Recent television includes: *Casualty*, *Reverse Psychology*, *Coronation Street*, *Grease Monkeys*, *Doctors And Nurses*, *Innocents*, *Dalziel And Pascoe*, *Holby City*, *Dream Team*, *Amongst Barbarians*, *Trial And Retribution*, *McCallum*, *Fighting Back*, *Inspector Alleyn*, *The Rector's*

Wife, *Tygo Road*, *Cardiac Arrest*, *Shalom Salaam*, *Black And Blue*, *Medics*, *Boon*, *This Office Life*, *The Bill*, *South Of The Border*, *King And Castle*, *Tandoori Nights*, *Old Men At The Zoo*, *Maybury*, *Minder*, *Target*, *The Road To 1984*, *Blunt Instrument*, *Cold Warrior*, *Sarah*, *Looking For Clancy*, *The Regiment*, *Imperial Palace*, *Adam Smith*, *The Brahmin Widow*, *First Lady*, *Moonbase 3*, *Doctor Who*, *Anything But The Woods*, *Rogue's Rock*, *The Moonstone* and *Uncle Tulip*.

Madhav also directs in the theatre, and has appeared in numerous films and radio plays.

Harvey Virdi Teetee

Harvey trained at the Academy Drama School.
Theatre credits include: Maria in *Twelfth Night* (Albery Theatre); Esther in *Calcutta Kosher* (Kali Theatre Company); Mrs Peachum in *The Threepenny Opera* (National Theatre); *Hijra* (West Yorkshire Playhouse); *14 Songs, 2 Weddings And A Funeral*, *A Tainted Dawn* and *A Yearning* (Tamasha Theatre Company); *Two Old Ladies*, *When We Are Married*, the Nurse in *Romeo And Juliet* and *Playboy Of The Asian World* (Leicester Haymarket); *Airport 2000* (Rif-Co/Leicester Haymarket); *Exodus* (Tara Arts); *Staying On* (Theatre Of Comedy tour); *Bravely Fought The Queen* (Border Crossings); *Magic Mirrors* (Quicksilver) and Juliet in *Romeo And Juliet* (Soapbox Theatre Company).
Television credits include: *Doctors*, *Whose Baby?*, *Cherished*, *Rose And Maloney*, *Hear The Silence*, *Boohbah*, *The House Across The Street*, *Baddiel Syndrome*, *Staying Alive*, *The Bill* and *Casualty*.
Film credits include: *Thunderbirds*, *Bride And Prejudice*, *Bend It Like Beckham*, *Anita And Me*, *Gran* and *Guru In Seven*.
Radio credits include: *A Good Match*, *Singh Tangos*, *Shakti*, *Dancing Girls Of Lahore*, *A Yearning* and *Samsara* (all for BBC Radio 4).

Pooja Kumar Polly

Pooja trained at LAMDA where she received the Cameron Mackintosh Bursary Award.
Theatre credits include: Maria in *Twelfth Night* and Puck, Bottom and Demetrius in *A Midsummer Night's Dream* (Theatre Royal Bath); Sabha in *Paradise* (Birmingham Repertory Theatre); Ursula in *The Learning Curve*, Dhadi in *Chale Ga, Chale Ga* and Amrit in *Best Of Both Worlds* (Women's Theatre); Mowgli in *The Jungle Book* (Tobacco Factory); Princess Belle in *Sleeping Beauty* (Tell-Tale Productions); Sukhbinder in *In The Dark* (Studio 3 Arts); Catherine in *A View From The Bridge* (Theatre Royal Bath Education) and Sathi in *Made In India* (Hangama Productions/Leicester Haymarket).
Television includes: *Casualty, Make My Day, TLC* and *The Day I Died*.

Creatives

Gurpreet Kaur Bhatti Writer

Gurpreet Kaur Bhatti's first play *Behsharam (Shameless)* broke box office records when it played at Soho Theatre and Birmingham Repertory Theatre in 2001. She has just written *The Cleaner*, an hour-long film for BBC1 and her first feature film *Pound Shop Boys* (originally commissioned by October Films/Film Council and developed through PAL). She is now working on commissions for the Royal Exchange Theatre Manchester, Kali Theatre and Maya Productions as well as developing a police drama series with Great Meadow Productions.
Other credits include the half hour film *Dead Meat*, produced by Channel 4 as part of the Dogma TV season; *Mera Des (My Country)*, a fifty minute play for Radio 3; *Pile Up* and *The Bride* (both commissioned serials for Carlton Television); *Londonee* (Theatre Royal Stratford East – rehearsed reading); *Two Old Ladies* (Leicester Haymarket); over thirty episodes of the BBC World Service Drama Serial *Westway*; and nine episodes of *EastEnders*.
Gurpreet studied Modern Languages at Bristol University and has worked as a journalist, refuge worker and actress. She has worked extensively with young people and community groups and is also a part-time carer.

Janet Steel Director

Janet began her career in theatre as an actress, appearing in many theatre, television and radio productions.
Theatre includes: *Cinders*, *A Colder Climate* (Royal Court); *Blood Wedding* (Half Moon); *Romeo And Juliet* (Sherman Theatre and Albany Empire) and *Oedipus Rex* (Tara Arts).
Television includes: *An English Christmas*, *The Bride*, *Gems*, *The Refuge* and *Shalom Salaam*.
Janet began her directing career as an assistant to Tessa Schneideman and The Loose Change Theatre Company. They produced UK premieres by renowned Spanish authors at BAC, which was where Janet directed her first full length piece, *White Biting Dog* by Judith Thompson.
Directing credits include: *April In Paris, Bretevski Street, A Hard Rain* and *Top Girls* (The Royal Theatre, Northampton); *Exodus*, as part of the Millennium Mysteries (Belgrade Coventry); Brecht's *Antigone And The Mother*, *Orpheus Descending, An Ideal Husband, Romeo And Juliet, The Knockey* and *Serious Money* (Rose Bruford College). In 2003 Janet became Artistic Director of Kali Theatre Company and for them has directed *Sock 'Em With Honey*, by Bapsi Sidhwa and *Calcutta Kosher* by Shelley Silas. Janet was recently awarded an MA with Distinction in Theatre Practices, from Rose Bruford College.

Matthew Wright Designer

Matthew trained at the Glasgow School of Art in Textile Design. Designs for theatre include *Clouds* (No 1 tour); *Us And Them* and *The Dead Eye Boy* (Hampstead); *Summer Lightning, Amy's View* (& Salisbury), *Arcadia* (Theatre Royal Northampton); *The Green Man* (Theatre Royal Plymouth/Bush Theatre); *Private Lives* and *Charley's Aunt* (Northcott Exeter); *Larkin With Women* (West Yorkshire Playhouse); *Four Nights In Knaresborough, All That Trouble We Had* (New Vic, Stoke); *Royal Supreme, Blood Red Saffron Yellow, Musik* and *The Imposter* (Theatre Royal Plymouth); *The Deep Blue Sea, Neville's Island* and *A Taste Of Honey* (Watford Palace); *Charley's Aunt* (Watford/Southampton); *Confusions* and *Habeus Corpus* (Salisbury); *Summer Lightning* (Salisbury & Theatre Royal Bath); *End Of The Affair* (Salisbury/Bridewell); *Our Country's Good* (Edinburgh Lyceum); *Hamlet* (RNT Education); *Woman In Mind* (Theatre Royal York); *Twelfth Night* and *Hamlet* (Oxford Stage Company); *Romeo And Juliet* (Greenwich/tour) and *Pow!* (Paines Plough).

Opera credits include *Ii Pomo D'oro* (Batignano Opera Festival) and *Don Pasquale* (Scottish Opera Go Round). He also designed the costumes for *Seriously Funny* for Channel Four Television.

He designed *Getting To The Foot Of The Mountain* and *Swamp City* for Birmingham Repertory Theatre.

Mark Doubleday Lighting Designer

Mark Doubleday was trained at LAMDA, where he won the Richard Pilbrow prize. Since then he has lit over 200 productions in most of the UK's regional theatres, as well as in Europe, USA, India, South East Asia and South America.

Most recent productions include: *Eugene Onegen* (MTL); *Le Nozze Di Figaro* (Opera Zuid, Netherlands); *Hansel And Gretel* (Scottish Opera Go Round); *Manon* and *Die Fledermaus* (English Touring Opera); *The Beggar's Opera, A Chorus Of Disapproval* and *Henry IV parts I & II* (Bristol Old Vic); *Falstaff* (RAM); *Ariadne Auf Naxos* (Aldeburgh); *Le Toreador, Messalina, Amadigi Di Gaula* and *I Giardini Della Storia* (Batignano); *Die Entfurung Aus Dem Serail* (Lackoslott Oper, Sweden); *A Nitro At The Opera* (ROH2); *Six Pack* (Tête à Tête/ENO Studio) and *Family Matters* (a newly commissioned opera, also for Tête à Tête), *La Fanciulla Del West* and *Norma* (Opera Holland Park); *Shadow Of A Gunman* (Tricycle Theatre).

Future plans include: *Rape Of Lucretia* (RCM) and *Revival* (ROH2).

^{THE}REP
Birmingham Repertory Theatre

Birmingham Repertory Theatre is one of Britain's leading national theatre companies. From its base in Birmingham, The REP produces over twenty new productions each year. Under the Artistic Direction of Jonathan Church, The REP is enjoying great success with a busy and exciting programme.

Over the last few years The REP's productions have included David Hare's trilogy of plays (*Racing Demon*, *Murmuring Judges* and *The Absence of War*), Steinbeck's *Of Mice And Men*, Miller's *A View From The Bridge*, *The Wizard Of Oz*, Ibsen's *A Doll's House* and the world premieres of Alistair Beaton's *Follow My Leader* and Simon Gray's *The Old Masters*. This Autumn has seen new productions of Fernando De Rojas's *Celestina*, directed by Calixto Bieito in association with Edinburgh International Festival, and Arthur Miller's *The Crucible*, which has just completed a national tour. Christmas 2004 will see a new production of Roald Dahl's *The Witches* as well as the return of The REP's original production of *The Snowman*, which has been delighting audiences in the West End for many years.

The commissioning and production of new work lies at the core of The REP's programme. In 1998 the company launched The Door, a venue exclusively dedicated to the production and presentation of new work. In 2004, The REP won the Peggy Ramsey Award, which will support the continuing development and commissioning of writers. One example of this is the world premiere of a new black comedy *Behzti (Dishonour)* by Gurpreet Kaur Bhatti: her critically-acclaimed first play *Behsharam (Shameless)* played to full houses in both The Door and Soho Theatre in London.

Developing new and particularly younger audiences is also at the heart of The REP's work, in its various Education initiatives, such as Transmissions, The Young REP, Page To Stage, as well as with the programming of work in The Door for children.

Birmingham Repertory Theatre productions regularly transfer to London and tour nationally and internationally. The REP's acclaimed production of Steinbeck's *Of Mice And Men* opened in the West End in 2003. Last year's collaboration with the Edinburgh International Festival – *Hamlet,* directed by Calixto Bieito, toured to Barcelona and Dublin following performances at the festival and in Birmingham. Previous productions that have been seen in London in recent years include *The Old Masters, Snowman, Fuddy Meers, Two Pianos, Four Hands, Baby Doll, My Best Friend, Terracotta, The Gift, A Wedding Story, Out In The Open, Tender, Behsharam (Shameless)* and *The Ramayana.*

Artistic Director **Jonathan Church**
Executive Director **Stuart Rogers**
Associate Director (Literary) **Ben Payne**

Box Office 0121 236 4455
Book online at www.birmingham-rep.co.uk

EUROPEAN COMMUNITY

European Regional
Development Fund

The Door

The Door was established six years ago as a theatre dedicated to the production and presentation of new writing. In this time, it has given world premieres to new plays from a new generation of British playwrights including Abi Morgan, Moira Buffini, Bryony Lavery, Crispin Whittell, Paul Lucas, Gurpreet Kaur Bhatti, Sarah Woods, Roy Williams, Kaite O'Reilly, Ray Grewal, Jess Walters, Jonathan Harvey, Tamsin Oglesby and Sarah Daniels. Last year, the company received The Peggy Ramsay Award for New Writing, which further supported the company's work in developing and commission new plays for the future. The programme of The Door aims to provide a distinct alternative to the work seen in the Main House theatre next door. It is a space where new voices and contemporary stories can be heard, and seeks to create new audiences for the work of the company in this city and beyond.

In addition to work by British writers, The Door has begun to develop collaborations with international companies and exchange new plays with theatres overseas. The company is working towards a festival of new writing in 2006 in collaboration with Teatro Kismet in Italy and Comédie de Valence in France to build on our co-production of *Through The Woods*, a new play for young people in French, Italian and English by Sarah Woods, which has now toured all three countries. Another long-term aim is to broaden the diversity of the work that we present and co-produce through developing relationships with a range of companies touring new writing, like Creative Origins, Kali, Graeae, and Yellow Earth theatre companies and the annual Fierce! Festival of new performance work.

The Door is also a place to explore new ideas and different approaches to making theatre, to develop new plays and support emerging companies – for example, through the theatre's *Beyond The Boundaries* project. It also emphasises work for and by young people, through *Transmissions* – our young playwright's project, our *First Stages* children's theatre programme and the strong emphasis on new work and work with living writers in *Young REP*, our youth theatre initiative.

For more information about the work of The Door or about our work with new writers, please contact Ben Payne or Caroline Jester at The REP on **0121 245 2000**.

Transmissions

Transmissions is The REP's unique project aimed at nurturing the playwrights of the future. It gives twenty young writers from across the West Midlands the chance to develop their writing skills in a constructive and creative way.

Transmissions writers are given the opportunity of working with professional playwrights to develop initial ideas into full and complete scripts.

The scheme allows participants to meet other writes in a fun and interactive environment, giving them the support and encouragement needed to expand their interest with a very definite aim: to see their work performed on stage by professional actors.

In July the writers come together with professional actors and directors to present a showcase of their work in the form of the Transmissions Festival.

Transmissions has a new outreach programme supported by the Paul Hamlyn Foundation, with schools from across the region participating. Professional playwrights lead workshops in schools, and extracts from plays developed by students are also performed in the summer festival in The Door.

"Transmissions hurtled into its second week, blazing with energy and delivering some of the most provocative and original new work to be seen anywhere in the city" Birmingham Post

"A rich and extraordinary assortment of tomorrow's talent" Evening Mail

"It is a brilliant enterprise" Birmingham Post

If you would like to become involved with Transmissions or want further information, please contact Caroline Jester in the Literary Department at The REP in **0121 245 2000**.

BEHZTI
(DISHONOUR)

First published in 2004 by Oberon Books Ltd
521 Caledonian Road, London N7 9RH
Tel: 020 7607 3637 / Fax: 020 7607 3629
e-mail: oberon.books@btinternet.com
www.oberonbooks.com

A catalogue record for this book is available from the British
Library.

ISBN: 1 84002 522 0

Cover photograph by Parenthesis

Printed in Great Britain by Antony Rowe Ltd, Chippenham

Contents

Foreword by Gurpreet Kaur Bhatti, 17

BEHZTI, 21

Glossary, 141

Foreword

Truth is everything in Sikhism, the truth of action, the truth of an individual, God's truth. The heritage of the Sikh people is one of courage and victory over adversity. Our leaders were brave revolutionaries with the finest minds, warriors who propagated values of egalitarianism and selflessness.

But sometimes I feel imprisoned by the mythology of the Sikh diaspora. We are apparently a living, breathing success story, breeding affluence through hard work and aspiration. There is certainly much to be proud of and our achievements and struggles have been extraordinary. They are a testament to our remarkable community – energetic, focused and able. But where there are winners there must be losers. And loss.

I find myself drawn to that which is beneath the surface of triumph. All that is anonymous and quiet, raging, despairing, human, inhumane, absurd and comical. To this and to those who are not beacons of multiculturalism, who live with fear and without hope and who thrive through their own versions of anti-social behaviour. I believe it is necessary for any community to keep evaluating its progress, to connect with its pain and to its past. And thus to cultivate a sense of humility and empathy: something much needed in our angry, dog-eat-dog times.

Clearly the fallibility of human nature means that the simple Sikh principles of equality, compassion and modesty are sometimes discarded in favour of outward appearance, wealth and the quest for power. I feel that distortion in practice must be confronted and our great ideals must be restored. Moreover, only by challenging fixed ideas of correct and incorrect behaviour can institutionalised hypocrisy be broken down. Often, those who err from the norm are condemned and marginalized, regardless of right or wrong, so that the community will survive. However, such survival is only for the fittest, and the weak are sometimes seen as unfortunates whose kismet is bad. Much store is set by ritual rooted in religion – though people's preoccupation with the external and not the internal often renders these rituals meaningless.

My play reflects these concerns. I believe that drama should be provocative and relevant. I wrote *Behzti* because I passionately oppose injustice and hypocrisy. And because writing drama allows me to create characters, stories, a world in which I, as an artist, can play and entertain and generate debate.

The writers I admire are courageous. They present their truths and dare to take risks whilst living with their fears. They tell us life is ferocious and terrifying, that we are imperfect and only when we embrace our imperfections honestly, can we have hope.

Such writers sometimes cause offence. But perhaps those who are affronted by the menace of dialogue and discussion, need to be offended.

The human spirit endures through the magic of storytelling. So let me tell you a story.

Gurpreet Bhatti
November 2004

My thanks to Janet Steel, Lindiwe Phahle, Cathy King, Roy Battersby, Michael Buffong, Amber Lone, Anne Edyvean, Manjeet Singh, Surinder Kaur Bhatti, Arun Arora, Sunil Lakhanpal, SAMPAD, everyone at The Birmingham REP and special thanks to Ben Payne.

Characters

BALBIR

MIN

ELVIS

GIANI JASWANT

MR SANDHU

TEETEE

POLLY

For Lindi, who guided me to the truth.
And who was the finest human being I have ever known.
I thank God for the gift of your soul, my beloved,
most treasured friend.

PROLOGUE
Bathing, Dressing And Eating

BALBIR KAUR, a Sikh woman in her late fifties, sits naked perched on a small stool in a bath. Her face is scarred with disappointment but her eyes are alive with ambition. There is a bucket of water and a plastic mug in front of her. She takes a mugful of water and pours it over her body. She looks around anxiously and shouts out. She speaks with a Punjabi accent.

BALBIR: No soap!

Silence. She looks around again.

No bloddy soap, shitter!

Silence. BALBIR pours another mugful of water over herself. MIN, a faithful but simple lump of lard, bustles in. She's a sturdy but ungainly ingénue, prone to outbursts of extreme excitability. MIN is dressed unfashionably in mismatched A line skirt, patterned blouse and pink trainers. Her uncombed hair is in bunches, and she looks younger than her 33 years. She hurriedly unwraps a new bar of household soap.

MIN: It was in the flipping fridge.

BALBIR: You want me to die.

MIN: Those chipolatas smell all carbolic now... I'm at sixes and sevens...

BALBIR: Before I have finished living.

MIN: Most probably butterflies.

MIN hands BALBIR the soap and refills the bucket. MIN goes to lather BALBIR's back and body.

BALBIR: Too hard!

MIN: Oh...shush up.

BALBIR: A lady must be soft. Always soft. Are you a lady or a fellow?

MIN: I'm a flipping well lady and you know it.

BALBIR: You look like a bloddy horse.

BALBIR points towards her vagina.

Polish here please.

MIN: You do it.

BALBIR: I intend to gleam upon my arrival. Make it spick and span!

MIN: Get lost.

BALBIR: That's where you came out of.

MIN: Don't be filthy. Not today.

BALBIR: Or was it my arse?

MIN: I'll wash your mouth out you mucky cow.

BALBIR chuckles as she washes herself.

BALBIR: I bet you eat soap.

MIN: I do not do silly things like that.

MIN pours water over her mother.

BALBIR: That's why you're so clean and shiny inside. Like a brand new penny. Nothing dirty's ever happened in there…

MIN: Flipping well get on with it, Elvis'll be here soon.

BALBIR: I told you to cancel that shitter. (*A beat.*) I want shampoo.

MIN: There's not time. And I've still got to get in the mood.

BALBIR: I'll do it.

BALBIR starts to get up.

MIN: Sit down!

BALBIR: You think Elizabeth Taylor leaves her abode without putting shampoo.

BALBIR rises slowly.

MIN: Don't!

BALBIR wobbles on her feet, she grabs a bottle of shampoo and proudly brandishes it around.

BALBIR: Look at me, look at me…

MIN's panicking. BALBIR squirts shampoo onto her hair.

MIN: Stop, I don't like it…

BALBIR teeters awkwardly, she's painfully unsteady on her feet. Shaking, she half works up a lather in her hair and giggles excitedly.

BALBIR: Yes…oh yes…look… I'm the king of the castle…all over again… The top kitty cat…

MIN reaches for her but BALBIR pushes her hand out of the way.

MIN: Please!

Suddenly BALBIR slips and falls, banging her arm. She shrieks as MIN swiftly catches her. There's a moment of disturbed silence. Mother and daughter breathe together quickly, fearfully. BALBIR screws up her face.

BALBIR: (*Low.*) Pain.

MIN: You silly sausage.

MIN rinses BALBIR's hair.

BALBIR: I don't want to die.

MIN: Don't depress yourself.

BALBIR starts to cry like a child. MIN beams encouragingly.

23

MIN: Guess what… I've only gone and booked us a taximan!

BALBIR: I mustn't die. Not yet.

MIN: Least you'll get to see heaven. (*A beat.*) Then again I suppose you might not.

BALBIR sobs. MIN holds her mother tightly to her significant breast. MIN then carefully wraps the towel around BALBIR and starts drying her body. After a moment, she skilfully lifts her up and places her onto a slender single bed, which is revealed to be next to the bath. Clothes are laid out at the back of the bed and there's an NHS commode next to it.

Arms up.

BALBIR complies. MIN picks up a plain white cotton slip from the back of the bed and puts it on her. This is a routine they know well.

BALBIR: I thought seeing as…it's today… I…I might wear a padded brassiere.

MIN: Knickers!

MIN searches around and finds a huge pair of white cotton pants. She dangles them in front of BALBIR who eyes them with disappointment.

BALBIR: Don't I have any frilly ones left?

MIN: You know you don't.

MIN puts the knickers to one side and finds a pot of extra strength E45 cream.

BALBIR: What am I supposed to do on a special occasion?

MIN: None of those left either.

MIN vigorously applies cream to her mother's legs and arms. Then MIN picks up BALBIR and carefully places her on the commode. BALBIR regards her with fury.

BALBIR: I don't want to.

MIN: Put your sensible hat on please.

BALBIR: Nothing's coming.

MIN: Just sit there for a minute.

> *MIN turns away and wraps a scarf around her head. She takes off her shoes and sits cross-legged on the floor. She clasps her hands together and starts a religious chant (Salokh). Her Punjabi is broken and her accent imperfect.*

> Thum Thakur, thum pay ardas, jiyo pind sabh theri ras…

BALBIR: What you doing that for?

MIN: Practice for later. I want to move my mouth in time with all the other Sikhs.

BALBIR: Those fat shitters.

MIN: You ought to join in. We want to give a good impression.

BALBIR: I'm having beef cobbler for my dinner.

MIN: Get lost. Cod in parsley or vegetarian.

BALBIR: Cobbler.

MIN: You shouldn't go there with cow's meat in your tummy.

> *Sound of trickling urine into the commode.*

> See.

BALBIR: I didn't want to. I made myself.

> *MIN gets up to wipe her mother and puts the knickers on her.*

> I am exercising control you see. Omnipotence.

> *MIN resumes her chanting as she lifts BALBIR back onto the bed. The chanting comes to an end.*

MIN: What does it mean?

BALBIR: Heh?

MIN: What I'm saying.

BALBIR: Who cares?

MIN: God! And me.

BALBIR: I told you before.

MIN: Again…

BALBIR: I want beef.

MIN: Mother…

BALBIR: Cobbler with gravy and duchess potatoes. I want it.

MIN: The devil'll take your soul away.

BALBIR: He's most welcome.

MIN hurries offstage.

Beef, naughty beef! Yippee.

Sound of a microwave being turned on offstage. MIN comes back in.

MIN: Tell me.

Exasperated BALBIR rolls her eyes and translates/talks double speed.

BALBIR: You are the Lord, to you we pray, Body and soul are your gifts to us, You are the mother and the father, we are your children, In your grace lies abundant peace, your bounds are beyond us, you are higher than the highest. The whole creation is threaded together through you, And abides in your Will, you alone know your mystery, Nanak your servant, is forever your sacrifice.

MIN: Is forever your sacrifice… (*MIN breathes in deeply as though she is smelling sweet flowers.*) … I love it. I love all that…hmmm…it's getting me all going…

BALBIR: Do my make up now.

MIN ignores her and produces a rickety old tape recorder.

Min!

MIN presses play on the tape recorder. 'Billie Jean' by Michael Jackson blares out. MIN starts to move her body in time with the music. With the freedom and energy of a child, she skips around and soaks up the rhythm. She dances joyfully but without much expertise.

Oh shitter…

MIN: Shush up!

She carries on dancing. BALBIR shouts over the music.

BALBIR: Rubbish…you look so rubbish…

MIN does the moonwalk rather brilliantly.

MIN: I'm not listening!

MIN carries on. The frenzy of her movement brings MIN close to hysteria.

Watch me mother…watch!

BALBIR crawls onto the floor and just about reaches the tape recorder. The song is coming to an end. She presses stop.

BALBIR: Help me.

Breathless MIN stands over her.

MIN: That was…absolutely outstanding… I feel…almost perfect. Like a royal blue slush puppy.

MIN walks away.

BALBIR: Please!

MIN slowly moves towards BALBIR as though she is about to pick her up, but instead tugs harshly at BALBIR's hair. BALBIR yelps with pain.

MIN: You don't interrupt. Not when I'm moving about.

BALBIR: That hurt. You hurt me.

MIN: You hurt people.

BALBIR: If I had a knife I'd stick it up your arse.

MIN: Oh shush up!

BALBIR: You're illegal.

MIN: Capital punishment is illegal but corporal isn't.

BALBIR: You are an evil person.

MIN: I'm trying not to be.

BALBIR: Criminal.

MIN helps BALBIR up.

MIN: Didn't even pull that hard.

BALBIR pretends to cry silently. MIN's knocked.

Come on…don't be unhappy… I'll say I'm sorry…

MIN gaily and genuinely yanks one of her bunches.

Look I'm doing it to myself. Now you've got your own back.

BALBIR isn't having it. MIN disappears under the bed and delves into a suitcase. She finds a shiny red and gold shalwar kameez, clearly suitable for a young woman. MIN endeavours to tantalise her mother with the suit.

How about this then?

BALBIR: Doesn't fit any more.

MIN: We'll squeeze you in. You'll be the belle of the ball.

BALBIR touches the material.

Imagine that. All those ladies, being jealous of you.

MIN carefully puts the shalwar on BALBIR.

BALBIR: What about my make up?

MIN finds blue eyeshadow and bright red lipstick in the suitcase. She hands them to BALBIR who with a quivering hand starts applying them badly to her face. MIN tidies up.

You should put some. You need it more than me.

MIN: I'm not bothering with that hokum.

BALBIR: You have to start. Otherwise you will never stop.

MIN: What?

BALBIR: Looking like a bloddy horse. (*A beat.*) Put some. Please.

MIN: Why?

BALBIR: Go on.

After a moment, MIN solemnly applies blue eyeshadow to her eyelids. BALBIR chuckles as she watches her.

And the lips, go on.

MIN applies the lipstick. MIN eyes herself in the compact mirror.

MIN: Doesn't look like me any more.

BALBIR: Thank bloddy God.

MIN: Suppose it's still me inside.

BALBIR: Nothing you can do about the insides.

BALBIR holds MIN's face in her hands. BALBIR smiles.

Yes, that is bit better. Now we have hope ducks, now we have hope.

MIN: Hope?

BALBIR: That the world is a big fat oyster, slimy and sticky in the hand. Always leaving some oyster optimism on the fingers.

MIN: Don't be mucky.

BALBIR: Hope that it is all still to come.

MIN: What's to come?

BALBIR: Sunbathing on the Riviera, balloon trips over Manhattan and cocktails till dawn with Richard Burton. That if you work hard and present your arguments with focus and precision, tomorrow will be another day.

MIN starts to pack a bag.

MIN: Shall I pack some extra pads in case your bladder can't cope?

BALBIR: You can keep your pads and pensions and prescriptions.

MIN: They're all for you.

BALBIR: I want long, silly, tipsy days with naughty men who shout and laugh. I want to play with glamorous bits and bobs that sparkle and twinkle.

MIN: Mother! Think about where we're going, think about the holy things that are written in the book.

BALBIR: I can't be bothered.

A microwave pings offstage.

MIN: You want to lend some attention to Guru Nanak.

MIN wheels out the commode.

BALBIR: Who is he? My dad?

MIN brings in a high chair and a ready meal for one.

MIN: He's our Jesus. And it's his day.

MIN helps BALBIR into the high chair and puts the meal in front of her.

You tuck in to your cobbler.

MIN heads out.

BALBIR: Min…

MIN: What?

BALBIR: Please do effort to look a bit more nice.

MIN: What flipping well for?

BALBIR: Please.

MIN looks away uneasily.

Min!

MIN: Alright!

MIN exits. BALBIR eats ravenously and every so often spits into a small bowl. She mutters to herself.

BALBIR: Mmm… Min…poor fatty Min… You should try the meat of the magnificent cow…they say I can't chew it but…look… (*She chews and then spits.*) …those lumpy molecules don't want to pass down my throat but I still get the effect of the red meat entering my blood, you see, I need my red blood flowing to be this living thing. You watch the juice inside me grab life by the scruff of its neck. I'll show those fat shitters what it is to transform into a creature of splendour and win the final battle of the war.

Unseen by BALBIR, a skinny young black man enters. This is ELVIS, BALBIR's home carer. He is in his twenties, gawky and gormless, but with razor-sharp edges. Carrying a zimmerframe with wheels, he listens to BALBIR as she eats.

Beef! Mincey, chewy, naughty, beefy beef! Makes you stronger than cod and parsley and vegetarian. And even if it turns my shit stinky doesn't matter. Only me is using my special toilet. You tell me to eat the Indian things but…so much taste is too much to tolerate.

ELVIS: You are disgusting, do you know that?

BALBIR: You are not supposed to come today.

ELVIS: Mouth like a rat's sewer.

ELVIS indicates the frame.

I've tightened the screws.

BALBIR: My purse.

ELVIS passes her a purse from under the pillow. He rolls the frame forward.

ELVIS: No more squeaks. See. You'll be floating like a butterfly. Whee…whee…

He pushes the frame in a circle around BALBIR. She takes a coin out of her purse and holds it out.

BALBIR: Take it.

ELVIS: Why?

BALBIR: For your birthday.

ELVIS: It's gone. Ages ago.

BALBIR: Is my present to you.

ELVIS: One pound?

BALBIR: Yes.

ELVIS: You know it's against the rules.

BALBIR: Take it and go.

ELVIS: I can't.

BALBIR: Please go.

ELVIS: We're off out soon.

BALBIR: You don't come.

ELVIS: I'm booked for the day. Time and a half.

BALBIR: If you go… I… I will let you kiss me…darling…

BALBIR offers up her lips. ELVIS recoils.

We won't tell the girl.

ELVIS picks up a hair dryer.

ELVIS: I'd actually rather not. Thanks all the same.

ELVIS starts drying BALBIR's hair. BALBIR screams.

BALBIR: Get out, get out of my house you shitter!

ELVIS carries on, unfazed by BALBIR's outburst. MIN comes back in.

Min, he's hitting me…

MIN: Elvis doesn't hit mother.

ELVIS turns off the hair dryer. MIN's wearing a simple shalwar kameez and looks rather fetching. She's carrying a pair of old tap shoes.

ELVIS: You look…quite radiant. If you don't mind me saying.

MIN picks up BALBIR's red and gold kameez.

MIN: Arms up.

BALBIR sticks her arms up. MIN and ELVIS put the top on BALBIR. It's a very tight squeeze.

BALBIR: He called me a smelly P.A.K.I.

MIN and ELVIS exchange a knowing glance. MIN sighs.

MIN: You stop your fibbing and finish that cobbler.

MIN sits on the floor and puts on the shoes. BALBIR attacks her food again. ELVIS starts styling BALBIR's hair. He indicates MIN's shoes.

ELVIS: Where did you get them?

MIN: Oxfam. She needed a new balaclava.

MIN starts to tap dance. BALBIR covers her ears. MIN dances without skill but manages to make a constant tap tap noise.

ELVIS: Hey…you're not bad…you've got potential.

MIN: Eh?

ELVIS: You know…like promise. I reckon you'll go far.

MIN: (*Breathless.*) Do you like the noise?

ELVIS: Yeah.

MIN: I love it.

ELVIS: You should go to a club.

MIN: Like a disco?

ELVIS: That's it.

MIN: We had them at school. You can't move in a disco, not like you can at home. Too many bodies and all them traffic lights going off at the same time. (*A beat.*) Ooh… I'm in the mood now.

MIN stops. With her hands on her hips she bends over like an athlete.

ELVIS: Hey…perhaps…I could take you.

BALBIR: (*Screams.*) No!

MIN: Don't you start a rumpus mother.

MIN takes off her shoes.

BALBIR: You know he doesn't have baths.

MIN: Tell her Elvis.

ELVIS: I wash myself every day.

BALBIR: And I said you to do effort.

MIN: I've tried.

ELVIS: She looks lovely.

BALBIR: You are sex maniac virgin, to you even bloddy horse is lovely.

MIN: Shush up!

ELVIS takes away BALBIR's plate and cutlery.

Please try and behave properly.

BALBIR: Send that shitter away.

MIN: I need him. I can't manage the frame and the chair on my own.

BALBIR: I will carry it all.

MIN: You can't wipe your own bottom.

BALBIR: Someone else, might aid us.

MIN: (*Shouts.*) There is no-one flipping else! Now shush up!

BALBIR retreats into herself and closes her eyes. ELVIS comes back in and wipes down BALBIR's high chair, he places a glass of water in front of her and ELVIS and MIN watch BALBIR fall asleep. They speak in hushed tones so as not to wake BALBIR.

ELVIS: You doing any more dancing?

MIN: No. I'm ready now.

ELVIS: Is there singing, in your church?

MIN: Yes…but you don't have to join in.

ELVIS: I'd rather.

MIN: You won't understand the words.

ELVIS: Then I'll hum. I need the practice.

MIN: Just get us in and out. You don't have to stay during.

ELVIS: I want to. Tell me what to do?

MIN: I can't really remember. Haven't been since I was little.

ELVIS: Thought you'd go every Sunday. See all your mates and that.

MIN: It's too much bother with the frame and the chair and her as well.

ELVIS: Don't her mates help?

MIN: Oh I don't like to make silly demands…

ELVIS: You should ask me.

MIN: Going out's not part of her package. I've had to make a special request.

ELVIS: I'd come anyway.

MIN: If you hold the frame, I'll push the chair.

ELVIS: I reckon you need more than fifteen minutes a day. I'll put in a word.

MIN: No, don't.

ELVIS: You shouldn't have to miss out on your culture.

MIN: She's never been interested before. This leaflet about Guruji's special day popped through the letterbox and she went all keen.

ELVIS: Tell me what it's like. In there.

MIN shakes her head helplessly.

Go on, you can do it.

MIN thinks hard.

MIN: You have to take your shoes off and cover your head.

ELVIS: Show me.

MIN giggles. She takes off her shoes and covers her head.

MIN: Then you go in and make sure you've got 2p in your hand or even a twenty.

She takes out a coin and holds it tightly in her hand.

You walk on the white sheets, there's women on one side and men on the other, but don't worry about them. (*She walks.*) Carry on straight towards the man with the beard, he'll be waving his wand, and the book's there in front of you.

ELVIS: Right.

MIN: You put your hands together (*She puts her hands together.*) and in that moment you have to think really quickly.

ELVIS: About what?

MIN: About God and what you want to say to him. Only don't speak it out loud, keep it deeply, deeply inside. (*She does the following action.*) You kneel down, look at the book, make sure your forehead touches the ground and then you whisper it, ever so quietly. Now get up, but don't turn your back on him, and go and sit down. It's best if you keep your legs crossed. He won't want to see your bits.

ELVIS: What do you want to say to him?

MIN: That…I love God and Guru Nanak and all the gurus and Jesus as well, very much, and I want to be a good disciple.

ELVIS: Do you have disciples then?

MIN: Of course.

ELVIS: How many?

MIN: I think…probably the same as you lot.

ELVIS: (*Hopeful.*) What else you gonna say?

MIN: Nothing.

ELVIS: Come on…there must be something more…

MIN: Er…that…he…might perhaps…show me the way through… Yes, that's it… So that things can stay. For me and her.

ELVIS: But things change.

MIN: Not necessarily. Change isn't always for the better Elvis.

ELVIS takes this in. MIN turns away uneasily.

Perhaps you wouldn't mind sorting out the chair?

ELVIS nods and turns to go.

Elvis!

He stops. MIN giggles nervously.

I feel funny…

ELVIS: Yeah?

MIN: All sort of…a bit…nervous… I'm not used to so many bodies.

ELVIS: You'll be alright.

MIN: Yes, I'm sure.

He turns to go again.

What if I get it wrong?

ELVIS nods to the ceiling.

ELVIS: He'll be watching over.

MIN: Thank you Elvis.

ELVIS exits. MIN gently shakes BALBIR to awaken her. MIN takes out a coat, a headscarf and a bag from under the bed. She puts them on the bed and then lifts her mother out of the chair. BALBIR stiffens her body.

What's the matter?

MIN just about manages to place her mother on the bed.

BALBIR: I don't want to go.

MIN: But I've done all the preparations now. I've worked myself up.

BALBIR: You go. On your own.

MIN: I can't…you know I can't. I've booked a taximan mother. I've even started to look forward… You're flipping well going.

BALBIR: Why does he have to come?

MIN: It's his job.

BALBIR: People will see us with him and think…

MIN: What?

BALBIR: That he is my son in law.

MIN: It's a new century, people understand about Social Services.

BALBIR: He'll spoil it.

MIN: We're going to pray and worship and be with our folk. Nothing can spoil that.

BALBIR: You don't care about me.

MIN: Don't you dare…

BALBIR: Only about yourself, you only bother about yourself.

MIN's getting to the end of her tether. She shouts.

MIN: Please, shush up.

BALBIR: I wish you'd never come out of me. I wish you'd never taken a breath and that I'd burnt you and buried you before anyone knew what a thicko you would turn out to be.

MIN: Don't call me that!

BALBIR: (*Chanting.*) Thicko…thicko…

MIN: I could have got CSEs….

BALBIR: Thickhead, thickhead…

MIN: And O-levels perhaps. I would have taken them as well if I hadn't had to keep bringing you down the hospital.

BALBIR: Thicko…thicko…thickhead…thickhead…Just like your black Elvis.

Almost in tears, MIN takes some sellotape out of a bag. She pulls some off and plasters it over BALBIR's mouth. BALBIR struggles, but MIN suppresses her.

MIN: You're forcing me. I'm only doing this because you are forcing me.

She puts two more rounds of sellotape over BALBIR's mouth and then ties her mother's wrists together.

I don't care what you say about me. But there's no need to be rude about other people.

BALBIR is finally silenced. MIN paces around, she speaks as though she is thinking very hard.

I'm trying mother. I'm trying. But sometimes I can't really cope very well, not in here and especially…

not…out there. And I know you seem to find Elvis…difficult and his presence deeply odious. But I derive a great deal of encouragement from him. That's how I manage. I should improve, that's true. I know I can do more and I will try. I promise. Maybe that's what I ought to say to God, that I'd like to be better. And perhaps he'll make me…turn me into something good and special, a thing to be proud of. (*A beat.*) But for now, for today, on this auspicious occasion of the birth of Guru Nanak, please let's put our trust and hope in God. (*A beat.*) And in Elvis.

BALBIR half nods.

I mean it.

BALBIR nods vigorously. MIN takes the sellotape off. BALBIR breathes out with relief.

BALBIR: Make sure you tell them he is not your boyfriend.

MIN: I don't do things like that.

BALBIR: Why don't you? Why don't you do things like that?

MIN: It's not me, you know I'm not a party person.

BALBIR: Then what person are you?

MIN: We'd better get our skates on.

BALBIR: After a certain age, a lady should not be on her own.

MIN: That's why I stay with you.

BALBIR: Forget me.

MIN: I can't.

BALBIR reaches for the headscarf and folds it into a triangle, she starts to put it on.

BALBIR: Today is my wedding anniversary.

MIN: (*Shocked.*) Oh mother.

BALBIR: In those times, girls used to be married in anticipation of the full moon, on the Guru's birthday.

MIN: How wonderfully romantic.

BALBIR: Now they get married on Saturdays and Sundays.

MIN: I didn't realise.

BALBIR: Before your father went, we used to imagine your wedding.

MIN: Was it like yours?

BALBIR: No. It was bigger and grander, hugely expensive and wildly flamboyant. Your groom would arrive on a white stallion, your body would drip in 24-carat gold, and you would be demure and expertly made up, the envy of all womanhood.

MIN: Me?

BALBIR: Like a photograph in a magazine. A moment of perfection, captured and held, to be remembered and yearned for, forever.

MIN: I know I'm a disappointment.

BALBIR: Yes. (*A beat.*) But it doesn't have to be that way. When we get there… I plan to ask Him Upstairs to bless us. Blessings are always granted on the Guruji's special day.

MIN: But you don't believe in God.

BALBIR: That doesn't stop him believing in me. (*A beat.*) You remember Mr Sandhu?

MIN: Did he used to have a curly perm?

BALBIR: I gather he wears a turban now.

MIN: Did my dad used to go on walks with him? In the park, while I rode my bike?

BALBIR: Possibly.

MIN: I can't ride a bike any more.

BALBIR: He is Chairman of the Gurdwara's Renovation Committee.

MIN: I thought he sold the pools.

BALBIR: Local councillor!

MIN: Done very well for himself.

BALBIR: You know he washed your father's body.

MIN: I don't have any vague recollections of anyone.

BALBIR: And he has always taken a great interest in me. And you.

MIN: He's never been round.

At this moment, unseen by MIN and BALBIR, ELVIS enters with the wheelchair.

BALBIR: A very busy person like that doesn't come round. (*A beat.*) When I detected his mobile telephone number on that leaflet, I rang it. He is going to aid us.

MIN: How?

BALBIR: He has a list. The cream of the cream of all lists.

MIN starts getting distressed.

MIN: I don't understand lists.

BALBIR: He is going to find someone for you.

MIN: Someone?

BALBIR: You will go to his office in the Gurdwara and talk to him.

MIN: I can't talk.

BALBIR: He will see what a nice young lady you are and he will match you up. And if you are a good girl, by this afternoon you might have a rich, handsome, successful fiancé.

MIN: You shouldn't have.

ELVIS can't bear any more.

ELVIS: Min!

BALBIR and MIN look round at him.

Do you want me to…wait downstairs for the taxi?

MIN: Yes please.

ELVIS retreats and exits.

BALBIR: I have to protect you from external forces. I must look after you.

MIN: But I look after you.

BALBIR: You are one of Nature's cruel jokes.

MIN: You've got nobody except me, remember that. And I won't leave you.

BALBIR: I will come with you. It will be a big property no doubt and I will have my own quarters. And when you bear your first son…

MIN: No…

BALBIR: I will be there to guide him through life's rocky road. And what a success he will be.

MIN: No mother, no. I won't.

BALBIR: This is something…perhaps the last thing I can do for you before they set me alight on a pauper's pyre.

MIN: No.

BALBIR: Finally there will be someone to…keep you company, instead of boring old me. Doesn't that sound…appealing?

MIN shakes her head.

Why?

MIN: Because it's not…it's not what's in my head.

BALBIR: What about what's between your legs?

MIN: Shush up!

BALBIR: You must have some womanly needs left? Please God tell me you have.

MIN: All that…all that's gone about me mother…it's lost…

BALBIR: You just have to carry on where you left off. What if we pretend you're doing your O-levels all over again…

MIN: They don't do O-levels any more.

BALBIR: If you just go and talk to him…

MIN veers between desperation and defiance.

MIN: I won't. I shall not.

This fuels BALBIR's fury.

BALBIR: You think you can say no to such a thing? You think a bloody horse like you can say no to Mr Sandhu?

MIN: I'm nothing to do with him.

BALBIR: He is trying to help you, to help us get out of this shitter hole your father left us in.

MIN: Don't you blame my dad, you're the one that ruins things.

BALBIR: He ruined me. And you. Embarrassing us, leaving us stinking of his dishonour…

MIN: It wasn't his fault. It wasn't him.

BALBIR: Your father flushed my life down the toilet.

MIN: You kept smacking him round the face!

BALBIR: He deserved it.

MIN's crying now. BALBIR feels for her.

Min! I know what sacrifices you've made.

MIN: I don't care about any of them.

BALBIR: It's because of me you've turned into this lump of lard, I know, and I'm sorry.

MIN: But I'm happy here…with you…

BALBIR: Only because you don't know anything else…because you have been imprisoned as my nursemaid.

MIN: Why can't you be happy as we are?

BALBIR: How? Eating plastic frozen school dinners, waiting for you to wipe my arse, being wheeled about like shopping in a supermarket trolley? You think it is pleasant watching a fat virgin become infertile? I want to live a life that is something. I want to be seen and noticed and invited by people. I want anything…that is not this.

MIN: I'm scared.

BALBIR: Of what.

MIN: Of all of it.

BALBIR: There isn't a brave bone in your body.

MIN: No.

BALBIR gets up using her frame and picks up her coat. She wobbles briefly but the familiar feel and support of the frame

gives her a certain confidence. She puts on the coat and eyes
MIN with disdain.

BALBIR: If I can show my face, you can open your mouth.
You're going to talk to Mr Sandhu, and if you're lucky
you'll end up with half a chance.

MIN: You won't make me mother. I do what I like and
there's nothing you can do about it.

BALBIR: We'll see.

MIN: I'm going to wish Guru Nanak a happy birthday and
that's all. He loves me and he's going to show me the
way.

BALBIR: And I want none of your bloddy dancing in front
of people. Always giving me the bloddy embarrassment.

MIN: (*Shouts.*) And you try not to poo yourself mother!

BALBIR wobbles but clutches her zimmerframe tightly and
stumbles out. MIN is left alone, sobbing. After a few moments,
she gets up, wipes away her tears, straightens herself out and
follows her mother outside.

Scene One
GURDWARA – Arrival

A vast dimly-lit empty space. This whole space may give rise to several
areas, but the significant action takes place centre stage. There is the
sense that parts of the space can be, or might turn into, anything.

Hypnotic Sikh religious music plays. On a square area, defined by
white sheets on the floor, sits one of the Gurdwara's priests, GIANI
JASWANT, 47, a pensive, heavy-hearted soul. He has a long black/
grey beard and wears a blue turban and a white kurtha pyjama. He
holds a stick of horse hair. GIANI JASWANT waves the stick about
and gently chants to the music.

At one side, an edgy, frightened-looking balding man throws darts at
a dartboard. Around the board is a variety of religious paraphernalia

(calendar, symbols, pictures) and above hangs an ornate kirpan (Sikh religious sword). This man is MR SANDHU, 55. Wearing a suit from Asda, he has a fastidious air and on first sight is utterly forgettable. There is a small desk and chair behind him. On the desk sits a turban as well as writing paper, a pen and a bag of mint humbugs. MR SANDHU nervously beholds the dart in his hand.

MR SANDHU: Double top…double top for a sweetie…

MR SANDHU throws the dart and quickly goes to retrieve it; as he wanders back he inserts a humbug into his mouth.

Lights reveal a small dank area centre stage. A shoe rack displays assorted footwear. POLLY DHODHAR, 48, a capable woman who's losing her once-sensational looks, sashays towards the rack. She wears a spangly shalwar kameez and carries a large shoulder bag. POLLY carefully inspects different shoes. Eventually she finds a pair of black patent stilettos. She briefly checks that no-one's looking and puts them on. She walks around in a circle, takes the shoes off, checks again that she's not being watched and hurriedly stuffs them in her bag. A hard-faced but curvaceous woman, TEETEE PARMAR, 52, approaches unseen by POLLY. She too carries a shoulder bag and shouts out angrily. Both women speak with broad Punjabi accents.

TEETEE: Joo naughty thief!

POLLY jumps. When she sees TEETEE, the two women burst into peals of laughter.

POLLY: Meh tha Darghi!

TEETEE starts looking through the shoes.

TEETEE: That bitch from the Post Office got Manolo Blahniks.

POLLY: I saw.

TEETEE: Probably took them in with her. Greedy cow.

They continue to rummage. TEETEE's getting frustrated.

All these cheapie people, coming to the Gurdwara in their stinking chappals they bought in 1973. Don't they have no respect for God?

POLLY finds some smart leather loafers.

POLLY: Patrick's Coxes!

TEETEE: Sure?

POLLY: Your size.

TEETEE eagerly puts them on. They fit perfectly. She walks about proudly.

TEETEE: Oh yes…this is more like it, very much more like it indeed. These are the foot holders of a queen, a goddess with a decent pair of trotters at the end of her tree trunks.

POLLY: Sandhu's daughter's.

TEETEE: That runt who vomits her parshad down the carsey?

She admires her feet. As they talk, POLLY and TEETEE try on different shoes from the rack.

TEETEE: Least daddy can buy her some new ones. Is she married yet?

POLLY: I heard she's a muff diver.

TEETEE: Someone'll still have her. (*A beat.*) Bet there'll be some proper decent shoes at that wedding.

POLLY: Your Billoo could do worse.

TEETEE: That stick insect can't handle one of mine.

POLLY: What's there to handle?

TEETEE: Billoo only likes big things. Big boobs, big bottoms, big houses, big cars…everything big…

POLLY: I like the sound of that.

TEETEE: And he has big ideas for his business. Expansion. He is buying a crane and a what you call it…scaffolding…oh and a tractor even…so you see he is not likely to mate with a lezzer.

POLLY: I thought I saw him up the dole.

TEETEE: He meets his uneducated friends there. He tries to direct those unlucky boys onto the right path. And then they go for chips.

POLLY reaches inside her bag.

POLLY: How proud you must be Teeteeji.

POLLY takes out a pamphlet of assorted paint colours and pointedly flicks through it.

TEETEE: I am but… I don't like to flaunt what I've got. What is that you are flicking Pollyji?

POLLY: Did I mention that while I was at the Cash and Carry, performing my weekly task for the Gurdwara, loading extra large bags of granulated sugar and 20-kilogram sacks of chappati flour, into my spacious Four by Four, I received a call on my mobile phone?

TEETEE: No.

POLLY: From Mr Sandhu…

TEETEE: No!

POLLY: Asking me to trawl the local DIY superstore for a pamphlet of assorted paint colours. He is apparently choosing a design scheme for the new extension to the Gurdwara.

TEETEE: Already?

POLLY: And judging by his amicable tone, I would not be surprised if he requested my opinion before making a final decision.

TEETEE: (*A beat.*) Do you want to know a big fat secret?

POLLY: Yes please.

TEETEE: Guess who will be building the new extension to the Gurdwara?

POLLY: That gora cowboy Thompson I expect.

TEETEE: (*Thrown.*) Who told you that?

POLLY: I saw his van parked outside yesterday. He was chewing his bacon roll with great confidence.

TEETEE: His confident chewing is about to be terminated. Guess again.

POLLY: Mr Sandhu is in charge of the new extension.

TEETEE: I know, but who will be building it?

POLLY: Not your Billoo?

TEETEE: And I am going to see Mr Sandhu later…

POLLY: No!

TEETEE: Because Billoo is making me his manager.

POLLY: No!

TEETEE: Yes! That boy is going to be extremely huge around these parts. You mark my words. He has a large brain and long fingers. Always a winning combination.

TEETEE stuffs a few pairs of shoes into POLLY's bag.

POLLY: (*Cheeky.*) You should tell him to come and visit me.

TEETEE: What?

POLLY: I could make him some aloo paratha to keep him fit and strong. (*A beat / sighs.*) No-one's tasted my aloo paratha in quite some time.

TEETEE grabs POLLY by the scruff of the neck and violently pushes her to the floor. TEETEE sits astride POLLY and tightens her grip around POLLY's throat.

(*Choking.*) Teeteeji!

TEETEE: You leave him alone. You don't go near my son, understand?

POLLY: I was joking, only joking.

TEETEE releases her.

TEETEE: Your jokes smell of dogshit.

POLLY composes herself.

Find some other boy to molest.

POLLY: (*Coughing.*) I've tried. They've all got blondie girlfriends.

They exchange a conciliatory smile. TEETEE sighs.

TEETEE: Today, I feel old.

POLLY: I don't. I feel damn well gorgeous.

TEETEE examines her hands.

TEETEE: I must have made a hundred rotis this morning.

POLLY: And I chopped a thousand onions.

In the worship area, GIANI JASWANT gets up and bows respectfully towards the holy book.

TEETEE: God will appreciate it, you will see.

GIANI JASWANT exits the worship area.

POLLY: (*Downbeat.*) Always we are just passing time. Over and over and over and over…

TEETEE playfully pokes POLLY in the ribs.

TEETEE: But what a time it is! All us ladies together, giving each other the company.

POLLY: (*Unsure.*) Yes.

TEETEE: So much fun God gives us, under his roof. We should be thankful.

GIANI JASWANT walks past. On seeing him, TEETEE adjusts her chooni (scarf), POLLY quickly greets him with a traditional Sikh Salutation.

POLLY: Sat siri akal Gianiji… Vaheguruji kha khalsa.

GIANI JASWANT responds half-heartedly.

GIANI: Vaheguruji khi fateh.

TEETEE: Very busy today Gianiji, you must be pleased.

POLLY: Like a church at Christmas.

TEETEE: All these people who only come to Gurdwara to fill their stomachs, have they no shame?

POLLY: God will show them.

There's an awkward silence.

TEETEE: Shall we bring you some chah Gianiji?

He shakes his head. They all stare at each other, not knowing what to say. The GIANI opens his mouth to speak, the ladies regard him with anticipation, it seems as though he is about to say something very important.

GIANI: I have been pondering…when a fly sits on an orange, it is up to the warrior to eat the pith. Then perhaps the dolphins will fly in the sky. It is only by such devotion that one can understand the true limitless power of the divine, enlightened one.

POLLY and TEETEE nod in bemused agreement.

POLLY: Perhaps you would like some methi dhi roti.

GIANI: No thank you. I prefer to arrange my own thali. Actually I was just on my way to relieve myself.

The GIANI heads off. Watching him go, POLLY turns to TEETEE.

POLLY: Bucharah, after so long, the drugs are still affecting his brain.

TEETEE: No-one was forcing him to put white powders up his nose.

POLLY: Still, he has had a hard life. You remember what it was like in that house…

TEETEE: Perhaps you should make him some aloo paratha.

POLLY: Giani Jaswant is far too old for me.

TEETEE: Stupid! He is at least two years younger than you.

POLLY: Exactly.

TEETEE gathers their things together.

Time to do more sayva?

TEETEE nods and releases a long suffering sigh. (Sayva, service to God, means helping out in the kitchen. The selfless and menial nature of this work is deemed to be an essential part of being a good Sikh.)

TEETEE: God is waiting. (*A beat.*) And that Binder Kaur always leaves her gold on the side when she's stirring the kheer.

The women laugh and go to leave when ELVIS enters (carrying BALBIR's bag and frame) followed by MIN who pushes BALBIR in her wheelchair. POLLY and TEETEE stop in their tracks, frozen by shock. They both stare at BALBIR who stares back. Moments pass. ELVIS and MIN don't know what to do, so stand awkwardly and look to the ground. BALBIR starts to gently sing a traditional, poignant bridal farewell (bidhai).

BALBIR: Babel bidya carendea menoo rakleh aaj dee rath veh.

Kiken rukha beti mehria meh sujan sudahleh app.

(Please father let me stay at home for just one more night.

How can I daughter? I've asked them to take you away.)

TEETEE joins in, softly, almost as if she's on automatic.

BALBIR / TEETEE: Theri melah dhi bich bich veh, doli meeri nay nungdee.

Ick itt cudvahdeh mangat beti car jah aap dhi.

(I can't leave father, my doli won't pass through your door.

Then I'll take this wall apart, brick by brick, until you can pass, go now daughter to your new home.)

BALBIR points a finger at POLLY and chuckles warmly.

BALBIR: You remember?

POLLY's eyes well with tears. She nods and drops to her knees, throwing her arms lovingly around BALBIR's legs. BALBIR turns to MIN and indicates POLLY.

You think you have seen beauty?

No response. BALBIR shouts.

You think you have seen beauty?

MIN: (*Anxious.*) I don't know.

BALBIR: Well you bloddy haven't. None of you bloddy lot have. Not ever. Not like this one on her wedding day. Nineteen she was. We sang that song and we sent her on her way...and we sobbed and we wailed. She was the jewel in our crown, our Audrey Hepburn. The skin, the eyes, the hair, the figure. Bloddy shitter, if she possessed a swimsuit she would have won Miss World.

BALBIR eyes TEETEE.

You remember that day Teetee Parmar?

Silence. TEETEE nods and puts her arms around BALBIR.

TEETEE: (*Emotional.*) We have missed you Bhanji.

POLLY: You are a mother to us Bhanji.

TEETEE: More than a mother.

POLLY: So missed you have been.

TEETEE indicates MIN.

TEETEE: This must be…

POLLY: Yes! How big she has become.

TEETEE: She used to be a girl, now she is a woman.

An intrigued POLLY regards ELVIS.

POLLY: And this…

TEETEE: Must be her friend.

BALBIR: No…he is our help…you understand…

ELVIS: I'm Elvis.

POLLY: That's what they all say.

TEETEE and POLLY laugh heartily. BALBIR joins in. The three women embrace and hold hands. MIN and ELVIS take off their shoes. BALBIR proudly indicates the women to MIN.

BALBIR: Say hello Maninder!

MIN: Oh…hello there.

BALBIR: When your poor useless father brought me to this country, we purchased a filthy, crumbling end of terrace…

TEETEE: Me and my old man lived in the cellar.

POLLY: And I lived in the cellar of the cellar, until I was married…

BALBIR: What days they were!

TEETEE: Bringing the coal in from outside…

BALBIR: Boiling the men's underwear…

POLLY: No carpet and no television…

TEETEE: Being spat at by little goreh children…

POLLY: Carrying big shiny handbags…

BALBIR: Big plops of rain falling through the ceiling…

TEETEE: Always some beating and shouting coming from one room or another…

POLLY: No proper food…

BALBIR: Bloddy marvellous days…

POLLY: (*To MIN.*) You used to do dancing for us.

MIN: I still can!

TEETEE: So pretty you were.

MIN: At school, they used to say I looked like a buffalo.

Embarrassed laughter. MIN goes to take off BALBIR's shoes.

POLLY: So lucky to have this kind of daughter Bhanji.

TEETEE: God will bless her. Not every girl would make such a sacrifice.

POLLY: And we miss her daddy so much. He is in our hearts and souls every second of every moment…

TEETEE: Who can believe that such a thing would happen…

BALBIR: (*Interrupts.*) Time to think of the future now.

TEETEE: It is up to God.

POLLY: Up to him.

TEETEE: You still have the toilet trouble Bhanji?

BALBIR: I grow stronger every day. You see I am not over yet. Plenty more pages of my story to be fingered. And you?

TEETEE: Oh I have been lucky. Blessed by good fortune and three sons. Strong as oxes, they are rich, playboy businessmen.

BALBIR: The old man?

TEETEE: Building a kauthi back home. He draws pictures of all the rooms in those blue airmail letters. When he finds a pen.

BALBIR: And your husband Pollyji?

POLLY: Dead as a doorknob… Heart attack… Sudden it was.

BALBIR: No-one told me.

Awkward silence.

TEETEE: But…I phoned you and left a message.

POLLY: I am alright now.

BALBIR: Really?

POLLY: (*Low.*) No.

TEETEE: Oh I am one hundred and ten per cent positive.

BALBIR: Of course. Maninder forgets things sometimes.

MIN: When?

POLLY: We wept very hard.

BALBIR: I am sorry Pollyji, I would like to have joined in with your weeping.

MIN: Perhaps I did forget.

TEETEE: You are only human.

MIN: (*Excited.*) You'll have to come round one day. I'll make a ginormous pan of sweet milky tea.

POLLY: We will come. One day.

MIN: I'll buy new biscuits to mark the occasion.

She takes a pen and paper out of her pocket and starts writing.

Ours is the tallest block on the estate. It's four pound fifty with a taximan.

BALBIR: They know the way.

MIN: But they've never been.

BALBIR grabs the paper from MIN and tosses it aside.

TEETEE: (*Uneasy.*) Bhanji, you know we are thinking about you and remembering you every day of our lives.

BALBIR: Sisters…you do not have to explain.

POLLY: (*Sad.*) But always God is keeping us so damn well busy.

BALBIR: You do not have to explain!

TEETEE: I am pushing the tea trolley around the hospital.

POLLY: I am packaging the airport food.

TEETEE: And then God calls us here.

POLLY: To do his never-ending work.

BALBIR: Of course! Maninder, tell the boy to get ready…

MIN: (*Harsh.*) Elvis mother!

MIN joins ELVIS, they organise BALBIR's stuff and set up her frame.

BALBIR: So many things have changed…over the years. Who would have thought…

POLLY: Yes.

BALBIR: You must tell me, things… I have been starved of things you see.

TEETEE: Oh yes.

BALBIR: What of my husband's dearest friend?

POLLY: A great success.

TEETEE: He has an office here now. Where he conducts affairs.

POLLY: Without Mr Sandhu, the Gurdwara would have no stainless steel utensils.

BALBIR: And the house? What has he done with my old house?

TEETEE: Converted into penthouse apartments. He rents them out.

POLLY: To students and DSS claimants. Did you know his little brother is now the head Giani at the Gurdwara?

Lights reveal an immobile GIANI JASWANT sitting on a toilet, clutching a stainless steel thali.

BALBIR: Jaswant?

GIANI JASWANT slowly eats from the thali.

But he was a most ungodly individual.

TEETEE: Yes.

BALBIR: (*A beat.*) I would…like to see our esteemed Beerji.

POLLY: Do you have an appointment?

BALBIR: No.

TEETEE: You know what he is?

BALBIR: I know. Can you take me to him?

POLLY: You need a visa to see Mr Sandhu.

BALBIR: Just point me in the right direction.

TEETEE: Do you have some…special business Bhanji?

BALBIR: (*A beat.*) The girl you see…she is in need of help.

TEETEE: Help?

BALBIR: I understand he has a list.

Silence.

TEETEE: Are you sure Bhanji…that that is what you want for her?

BALBIR: Oh yes. The old ways never did us any harm.

TEETEE: No.

BALBIR: So shall we go?

MIN and ELVIS approach with BALBIR's frame and things.

MIN: (*To ELVIS.*) Where's your baseball cap?

ELVIS: I left it.

TEETEE: You have to cover your head…

POLLY: …before you enter God's house.

BALBIR: He doesn't understand.

TEETEE rummages in her bag.

TEETEE: Lucky I have something spare.

She takes out a patterned floral ladies' headscarf.

ELVIS: What's that for?

TEETEE and POLLY tie the headscarf round ELVIS' head in the typical way Sikh men tie scarves to cover their heads before entering a religious space. ELVIS tears himself away.

Oy get off. I ain't a woman.

MIN: They're normally white hankies.

ELVIS: I ain't wearing that.

TEETEE: Please do not insult our culture.

BALBIR: Put it!

MIN: You have to have something.

> *Seeing MIN's imploring face, ELVIS slowly moves towards the women. POLLY ties the scarf on him.*

POLLY: Now he is Elvis Singh.

> *POLLY and TEETEE clap their hands to do a gidha (traditional folk dance).*

TEETEE: (*Chants.*) One for the money, two for the show.

> *They dance around ELVIS, clap and make blowing, spitting sounds with their mouths (part of the gidha).*

MIN: Don't!

> *ELVIS angrily tears off the scarf.*

ELVIS: Stop it right.

POLLY: Oh Elvis…

ELVIS: I ain't here for no-one's amusement!

POLLY: We were only playing.

BALBIR: He doesn't understand playing.

TEETEE: Such anger! It is not usual to see such anger in the Gurdwara.

BALBIR: Rest assured ladies, I will be making a comprehensive complaint to the relevant authorities.

POLLY: No Bhanji…it is our sillibilliness…we are sorry Elvis…

> *MIN nods nervously at ELVIS.*

POLLY: Come with me and I will find you a spare scarf.

ELVIS: I'm staying here.

POLLY: All the men borrow them.

MIN: Go on.

ELVIS: I'm not supposed to leave you. What if something happens?

MIN: We'll see you inside in a minute. Please.

ELVIS reluctantly heads off with POLLY. MIN goes to lift BALBIR out of her wheelchair.

Let's venture forth mother.

BALBIR: Not yet.

BALBIR gets up and holds onto her frame, she wobbles towards TEETEE.

Any hunks hang round the gurdwara Teeteeji?

TEETEE: I wouldn't know.

BALBIR: How about you and me go for a wander?

TEETEE: (*Reluctant.*) Bhanji…

BALBIR: Let's see who we bump into…for old times' sake…

MIN: Mother! Stop bothering the nice lady.

BALBIR moves closer to TEETEE out of MIN's earshot.

BALBIR: (*Clipped.*) After all these years, don't you think you owe me a bloddy wander?

TEETEE picks up her bag and turns to MIN.

TEETEE: You!

MIN: What?

TEETEE: I am taking your mummy for a walk.

MIN: You can't.

TEETEE goes off.

BALBIR: Shut up shitter!

In the background, GIANI JASWANT gets up from the toilet. Using her frame, BALBIR follows TEETEE.

MIN: *(Fearful.)* What am I supposed to do?

MIN looks around nervously. She spots GIANI JASWANT walking to the kitchen area. She follows him.

Scene Two
GURDWARA – Covering the head

POLLY and ELVIS stand in front of a large, open petthi (Indian trunk). POLLY takes out a pink turban.

ELVIS: No.

POLLY: Why?

ELVIS: I'm not a Sikh am I?

POLLY: Try it. For fun.

She puts it on his head.

(Admiring.) Very handsome.

ELVIS: I'm not.

POLLY: You look like a bridegroom, burning with passion, hungry for his ravishing bride.

ELVIS quickly takes the turban off.

ELVIS: Can I have one of them scarves?

POLLY continues to rummage.

POLLY: You are their helper?

ELVIS: Home care. From Social Services. I heat her dinner up and wash the plates. And do odd jobs like… I bring shopping round if Min can't carry it and I comb her mum's hair most days. Usually I've only got fifteen minutes but I try and stay longer.

POLLY: Do you care for other people?

ELVIS: Mostly old folks. I shave and wash and wipe them till they look like million dollar grannies and granddads.

POLLY: Very nice. And what does your girlfriend do?

ELVIS: I ain't got a girl.

POLLY: Single?

ELVIS nods.

Like me. (*A beat.*) Tell me, these days how does one meet people?

ELVIS: How do you mean?

POLLY: You know…a gentleman…and a lady…

ELVIS: Er… I dunno…down the pub, or in shops or at bus stops?

POLLY: How lovely to have such…opportunities.

ELVIS: Oh I don't. But that's what people do, I reckon.

POLLY: You know… I am not a racialist.

ELVIS: Good.

POLLY: And my husband…well he was an open-minded man.

ELVIS: Can I please have one of them scarves?

POLLY: You're in a rush.

ELVIS: I've got to get back… I'm supposed to be responsible.

POLLY puts a white headscarf on ELVIS. They can't take their eyes off each other and this moment is loaded with sexual tension. It sizzles, silently.

ELVIS: You must miss him.

POLLY: Deeply. I miss him deeply.

ELVIS: I can see.

POLLY: Thank you. For seeing.

ELVIS: It's obvious.

POLLY: Not to everyone.

ELVIS: You wanna get out and about.

POLLY: I can't.

ELVIS: Why?

POLLY: It doesn't look…nice.

ELVIS: What?

POLLY: When he ended, so did I.

ELVIS: That don't sound right.

Silence. POLLY moves close to ELVIS.

POLLY: I just need to…

POLLY adjusts his scarf.

How does that feel?

ELVIS: Good.

POLLY: It looks…perfect…

They freeze for a moment and their faces move towards each other as though they're about to kiss. ELVIS hurriedly turns away.

ELVIS: I'd better get back. Thanks yeah.

POLLY: Stay a bit.

ELVIS: She needs me.

POLLY: Elvis!

ELVIS: Yeah?

POLLY: What is your favourite colour?

ELVIS: Er…blue's…alright…

POLLY: Good choice.

> *ELVIS turns to go.*

Will I see you later?

> *ELVIS smiles at her cheerfully.*

ELVIS: I'm booked for the day.

> *He goes off. POLLY beams to herself excitedly, she takes out the paint pamphlet and flicks through it. She stops at a page of blues.*

POLLY: (*Whispers / reads.*) Sapphire lagoon.

> *She gently places a hand on her heart.*

Scene Three
GURDWARA – Preparing for Mr Sandhu

MR SANDHU throws darts at the board as before. He goes to retrieve the darts and stuffs a handful of sweets into his mouth. TEETEE and BALBIR approach. A screen separates SANDHU's office area and he remains unseen by them. POLLY enters the worship area. She bows in front of the book and sits down cross-legged. She clasps her hands together and meditates. TEETEE nods towards the screen.

TEETEE: Through there.

BALBIR: A visa you say?

> *TEETEE doesn't respond. BALBIR regards the screen apprehensively.*

I mean we spoke on the phone, but it is always better to confirm in the flesh.

TEETEE: Yes.

BALBIR: And I must prepare him for the girl. You see…she is not your usual type of individual.

TEETEE: No.

BALBIR: He is a man who can make things happen, am I right?

TEETEE: Certainly.

BALBIR: We need ones like him. Doers. If only I had had one like him… Now quickly, do my make up…

TEETEE takes the make up out of BALBIR's bag and retouches BALBIR's face.

We must never let ourselves go.

TEETEE: Never.

BALBIR: It is good to see you Teetee.

TEETEE: And you Bhanji.

BALBIR: Thank God we are all still living up to our expectations.

TEETEE: Thank God.

BALBIR hobbles towards the screen. Suddenly TEETEE screams out.

Don't go in there!

BALBIR: Why not?

TEETEE: (*A beat.*) You…you…don't have an appointment.

BALBIR: (*Quiet.*) Do you remember who I am? What I was?

TEETEE: Bhanji…

BALBIR: (*Shouts.*) Bloody shitter, you used to scrub my floor and press my clothes and weep at my feet when all your thieving trash relatives murdered each other.

TEETEE: Yes.

BALBIR: All of you shitters, taking refuge under my roof. No murmurings or mutterings when the bricks and mortar slipped through my fingers and my name… (*Louder.*) My name was no longer spoken, instead ended up written in red ink on a pocket blue rent book.

TEETEE: I am sorry Bhanji for what you have endured.

BALBIR: You know you can't ever touch me Teetee… You can't ever, won't ever be Me. And you are jealous. Always jealous. You yearn for what I've got, what I've had, and you want that for yourself. You can't stand the idea of him helping me, wanting to help me. Can you?

TEETEE: No.

BALBIR: Always the same Teetee, spoiling the happiness of others.

TEETEE: Actually Bhanji… I was joking.

BALBIR takes this in.

BALBIR: (*A beat.*) So was I.

They smile at each other uneasily.

TEETEE: Wait a few moments, gather your thoughts, then knock loudly. Always best to enter such a room, prepared.

TEETEE turns to go.

He will be happy to see you.

TEETEE heads off. BALBIR beholds the screen anxiously. In the background ELVIS hovers around the shoe rack, he is clearly lost.

Scene Four
GURDWARA – God is Love

A stainless steel workstation. A sink and a pile of stainless steel utensils.

The GIANI eats a samosa. MIN stands at the sink and looks around. She approaches the GIANI.

MIN: Oh dear… Excuse me…sir…

She puts her hands together.

Sat siri akal…

He stares at her, unmoved.

MIN: What am I meant to do?

GIANI: What?

MIN: I don't know what I'm supposed to do. In here.

GIANI: Then you should find out.

MIN: That's why I'm asking you.

GIANI: Who am I?

MIN: A…person?

GIANI: I am an empty void, and know only of empty voids…if you want to ask a question…you must ask…

He points to the sky.

MIN: Is there anyone else about…who could tell me about such things?

GIANI: I try not to see people…or things. But sometimes I cannot prevent it.

Confused, MIN picks up some of the kitchen utensils.

MIN: Perhaps I'll do some washing up.

She starts washing up.

Are you one of those that waves the wand?

GIANI: You could say that.

MIN: Will you teach me a hymn?

GIANI: I don't teach... I am a learner still...

MIN: I bet you love God. A lot.

GIANI: I want...very badly...to serve him well.

MIN: So do I... Sir... Can you please tell me what is it exactly God wants?

The GIANI regards her, puzzled.

GIANI: I'm not sure about all that.

MIN: But you must have an idea.

GIANI: Why should I?

MIN: How about...one of his stories then?

Silence. The GIANI prepares himself to speak.

GIANI: All I know is this. Once upon a time there was a bedraggled man who woke up regularly in the front room of a small, abject house...in front of the test card as it happens...smelling. His mouth was always fixed around an empty bottle and there were tubes of five pound notes lying on mirrors all around... Ladies often left mugs of sweet milky tea by his side. They laughed and held their noses before slamming the door shut. This continued. Other men came and went but the bedraggled man had blurred vision and couldn't make much out. One day there was the sound of screaming and some kerfuffle about a body on a railway track. They pulled the bedraggled man out of the front room as they had to make way for a coffin. Someone gave him a fizzy potion and he fell asleep on a 747, which eventually came to a halt outside Indira Gandhi Airport. At the end of the GT road he found himself in a wheatfield and finally woke up. The village people hosed him down and brought him fresh saag and mackee dhi roti. They taught him to pray and he started wearing white cotton underwear. The man was no longer bedraggled and now God was happy. He had got what he wanted.

MIN stares at him, dumbstruck.

MIN: (*Slowly.*) That is flipping well brilliant!

GIANI: Excuse me please. I want to go to sleep now.

MIN: The begaggled man became…like a butterfly.

GIANI JASWANT lies down and closes his eye.

But suppose you haven't been…very good inside…for a very long time…and what if you can't…become a butterfly?

The GIANI doesn't respond.

Please…tell me…sir?

GIANI: You stay sleeping and smelling in the house.

The GIANI goes to sleep.

MIN: If you make God happy, does that mean you get good, sir?

ELVIS enters with BALBIR's wheelchair.

ELVIS: I've been looking for you everywhere! Where's Balbir?

MIN: Off praying with that kind lady.

ELVIS: I was worried.

MIN: Do you think a person can be different, from what he is Elvis?

ELVIS: Dunno… yeah…I think…I hope… Otherwise there'd never be any new days or times would there? Maybe that's what we all need, new days and times.

MIN: Perhaps you could give us a hymn while I do these cups.

ELVIS: Min…

MIN: (*Interrupts.*) I think God might like that Elvis.

Scene Five
GURDWARA – The Deal

BALBIR tentatively moves towards MR SANDHU's screen. She knocks. He immediately jumps and hurries to put on his turban.

SANDHU: Wait!

He sits down behind his desk. He frantically finds an old fashioned fountain pen and starts writing on a sheet of paper with meticulous precision.

Yes?

BALBIR wobbles in with her frame. She stops in front of his desk and grins. MR SANDHU looks up and regards her for a moment; he appears terrified.

Yes?

BALBIR: How is it going?

SANDHU is paralysed with shock.

Don't get up. I've been shown around already. I've been all over and I must say you've done a spectacular job with this place. Simply splendid. Whoever chose the carpet in the entry area is a genius. So very soft, but yet firm which is what the ball of the foot requires. And proper cotton sheets for a change, not those market ones that bobble. Were they from a department store?

SANDHU nods uncomfortably.

And the toilets are even clean. Of course there is the smell, but what do you expect from our people.

BALBIR indicates the Kirpan, she nods with approval.

A healthy reminder that we are a warrior race. Seventeenth century I suppose?

Again SANDHU nods. There's a difficult silence.

SANDHU: (*Nervous.*) I do not have any appointments today.

BALBIR: You are free then?

SANDHU: (*Shy.*) No-one is supposed to come.

BALBIR: Took me a while to find you. But I didn't let a couple of flights stop me! I pushed and pulled and yanked myself up. (*Deep breath.*) Like Hillary and Tensing when they reached the top of the world.

SANDHU: You are not supposed to be here. There are no appointments…today.

BALBIR: Oh… I thought… I…after we spoke on the phone, I supposed we had an…understanding.

SANDHU stares at BALBIR intently.

SANDHU: Please…who are you?

BALBIR: Oh…how silly of me…of course… I am not the… (*She means to say beauty but can't.*) …person…I once was, Sandhuji… beerji. I am…er…Tej's wife.

SANDHU: Tej?

BALBIR nods.

Tej?

BALBIR nods. SANDHU thinks hard.

He jumped out of that train.

SANDHU's mood starts to change. He starts to come into his own.

BALBIR: The man was endlessly irresponsible. But now there is the girl to think of.

SANDHU: I remember… Tej was taking pills.

BALBIR: You mentioned a list.

SANDHU: And he liked to drink pints of lager with a teaspoon in the Rose and Crown.

BALBIR: You said it was the cream of the cream.

SANDHU: Afterwards he'd have a whisky chaser.

BALBIR: The list…beerji… I thought you could help…

SANDHU: Yes. I do recall now.

BALBIR: Marvellous.

SANDHU: You know I haven't considered Tej for many years. And now suddenly I miss him. Terribly. I almost have a yearning for him.

BALBIR: You do?

SANDHU: He was always so very…

BALBIR: …drunk.

SANDHU: Yes he was, but he was far more than that. He was a soft man, gentle and quite shy.

BALBIR: The girl is in her prime. More or less.

SANDHU: Tell me about Tej's girl.

BALBIR: Sadly she has been lumbered with many of her father's attributes. And she's no spring chicken, but she has a certain something.

SANDHU: Does she resemble him?

BALBIR: Er…yes…and she is strangely vital. And…er… domesticated. Very reliable and honest also.

SANDHU: She wants someone?

BALBIR: From the list.

SANDHU: Boyfriends?

BALBIR: No such luck.

SANDHU: They all have boyfriends these days.

BALBIR: Not her. Never. Ever. At all.

SANDHU reaches for a book, which sits on his desk. It's the Sikh guide to first names. He puts on a pair of glasses.

SANDHU: She sounds...special.

BALBIR: Oh...she is.

SANDHU: What is her name?

BALBIR: Maninder.

SANDHU flicks through the book and stops at a page.

SANDHU: (*Reads.*) Maninder – Goddess of the soul. An inexact but charming translation. (*A beat.*) Tell me, does she desire love?

BALBIR: Oh yes.

SANDHU takes off his glasses.

SANDHU: Love. Love is a gift from God, the purest and yet most complex aspect of being. It makes you feel warm, exuberant, expansive and possible. (*He sighs.*) Ah...to give love...to receive love...to be blessed with a lover.

BALBIR: (*Unsure.*) Yes.

SANDHU: But a lover is not the one who is happy only in happy times and miserable in adversity. A lover is the one who is yours, who is inside you, who you are inside. Who makes you feel like hot chocolate sauce on milky vanilla ice cream or treacle sponge with extra thick double custard or pink roast lamb with thin garlicky juices and buttery jersey royals. Someone who makes you feel you are worth something…anything…who will let you play and fight and be simple. And who won't hate you. Ever. No matter how disgusting or disgraceful or shameful you really are. Someone who will wait. Not shout and stop everything, and never suppress the wanting. Who believes. (*A beat.*) To be bestowed with such a gift is truly excellent fortune.

Silence. BALBIR's rather taken aback. She thinks for a moment.

BALBIR: And how…er…is the lovely Madhu?

SANDHU: (*A beat.*) Having spent the afternoon in a seaweed body wrap, my wife came home one day and unfortunately…drank a bottle of Dettol.

BALBIR: Oh dear.

SANDHU: Needless to say, she expired.

BALBIR: Depression?

SANDHU: For a week or so, but I got over it.

BALBIR: I meant Madhu?

SANDHU: She seemed alright to me.

BALBIR: Such a sad story.

SANDHU: Tej…was my friend.

BALBIR: I remember.

SANDHU: Perhaps you should go now.

BALBIR: Go?

SANDHU: A man needs time to reflect.

BALBIR: (*A beat.*) I have been reflecting for twenty years. Dreaming of red and gold wallpaper in my front room. Burgundy velvet drapes, a white leather settee and an avocado green bathroom suite. You see I have come to realise that the time for reflection has passed. (*A beat.*) I hear you are something of a property magnate Sandhuji.

SANDHU: I do my best for my people.

BALBIR: I had plans once. Of entrepreneurship and empire. My husband squandered them.

SANDHU: Please do not speak of him harshly.

BALBIR: Before his ashes were flung over Brighton Pier, my home was taken away.

SANDHU: The property was about to be repossessed and the purchase ensured that Tej had a first class funeral. As I recall I managed the funds expertly and us men were able to give him a special send off at the Rose and Crown. Whisky chasers were served with pints of lager as a fitting tribute. George, the landlord, seemed most impressed.

BALBIR: I lost my place.

SANDHU: Luckily I fought for the names of his dependents to be inserted at the top of the Council's list.

BALBIR: Yet you have never visited our humble domicile?

SANDHU: I have such…painful recollections. Of his departure.

BALBIR: Of course. Our existence has been overwhelmed by the vile selfishness of my husband's pathetic act. If it were possible I too would obliterate myself and the girl from my own memory.

SANDHU: I have subsequently become accustomed to solitude.

BALBIR: Someone must now take charge of the girl. She and I were never compensated… So the list…beerji… you understand…

SANDHU: (*A beat.*) Has she ever had any physical…?

BALBIR: (*Interrupts.*) No!

SANDHU: A plus point.

BALBIR: I thought you should see her…so that an appropriate choice can be chosen.

SANDHU: Yes, I would like to meet Tej's girl.

BALBIR: When?

SANDHU: Tell her to go and pray first, but not to be too long.

BALBIR: (*Clipped.*) You know…fate has been immeasurably unkind to her.

SANDHU: (*A beat.*) Just like her father.

BALBIR hobbles out. Unseen by BALBIR, TEETEE watches her go. SANDHU takes off his turban and resumes his game of darts. TEETEE approaches the screen and knocks.

Scene Six
GURDWARA – A happy time before it

ELVIS and MIN are doing sayva – washing up glasses and pans at the stainless steel workstation. GIANI JASWANT is asleep as before. A beaming MIN is singing badly, but with the same exuberance she displayed when she was dancing.

MIN: You gave me a heart and you gave me a smile,
You gave me Jesus and you gave me a style.
But I just thank you Lord for making me Me!

ELVIS: What you singing about Jesus for?

MIN: Sounds nice. Your turn.

ELVIS clears his throat and starts to sing with beautiful gospel undertones. MIN claps along.

ELVIS: Precious Lord, take my hand, lead me on, let me stand, I am tired, I am weak, I am worn…
Through the storm, through the night, lead me on, to the light, take my hand, precious lord, lead me on.

MIN: Oooh…you got to love that.

ELVIS: Teach me one of yours.

MIN: I don't know any. Not properly.

ELVIS: You must…

MIN considers this and starts to chant.

MIN: Satnam, satnam, satnamji, vaheguru, vaheguru, vaheguruji, japo, satnam, satnam…

She continues, ELVIS joins in. The chant ends.

ELVIS: You look happy.

MIN: It's brilliant here.

ELVIS: What do you like about it?

MIN: All of it. Like when you wash up and clean in here, you're doing it for everyone. Not yourself. But you're still doing it because you want to.

ELVIS: (*Unsure.*) Right.

MIN: And the people around you, they're good. They do nice things and have friendly thoughts.

ELVIS: (*Tentative.*) Do you ever go out to other places?

MIN: Oh…yes…hospital, post office, chemist. Sometimes I buy clothes if there's a blue cross sale.

ELVIS: What about when it gets late?

MIN shakes her head awkwardly.

I'm in the pub most evenings. After the last granny's tucked up in bed and I've fed my dad, that's where you'll find me. I don't say much, I'm just there. Quiet, trying not to think about anything, cos I know tomorrow's gonna be just the same as today. Belter, that's the barman, he makes sure my glass is half full and sometimes when it's nearly closing time, when there's not been a broken window and Belter's not got his hands on a pair of schoolgirl tits, he tells me to get on the stage. And then it's my turn to shine.

Nervous, ELVIS moves closer to MIN.

If you like…I could bring you down there. One night.

MIN: How about…how about another song?

ELVIS nods. He starts singing Bob Marley's One Drop. Unseen by MIN and ELVIS, GIANI JASWANT gets up. Out of the blue, GIANI JASWANT joins in with the chorus. ELVIS is immediately silenced.

MIN: Sorry Sir.

ELVIS: I didn't mean no offence.

MIN: He's a Christian you see.

ELVIS: No I'm not.

MIN: He's not used to performing selfless service to God.

GIANI: There is no Christian or Hindu or Muslim or Jew or Buddhist or Rastafarian or Sikh.

MIN and ELVIS look at each other confused.

MIN: (*Whispers to ELVIS.*) What are we doing here then?

GIANI: Only the divine being. (*A beat.*) Ek Umkar, Satnam. (*A beat.*) Have you ever been to the Notting Hill Carnival?

ELVIS and MIN shake their heads.

You should go. It is free and you get to blow a whistle. I haven't been for many years, not since I started growing my hair. If you don't get stuck behind a float and manage to avoid the knife-wielding girl gangs and the ladies with sequinned bikini bottoms, it is possible to find the spirit of the Guru's unique illumination. From that experience of truth and enlightenment, one can come forth from the darkness and like an insect around a light bulb be exposed to the shining brightness of purity and wholeness.

MIN and ELVIS look on mystified. GIANI JASWANT takes a paratha lying on the side and munches on it.

In the company of saints and holy people
No more is there a feeling of 'us' and 'them'
No-one an enemy, none a stranger
I get along with all*

The GIANI exits.

ELVIS: I don't get it.

MIN: People like us aren't supposed to.

ELVIS: What?

MIN: We have to make do with listening to him.

ELVIS: Min…there's something I'd like to say to you…

MIN: Oh dear.

BALBIR staggers in.

ELVIS: But I'm not quite sure how to speak it…

BALBIR: Who loves you baby!

BALBIR stumbles to the floor.

MIN: Where's your lady?

MIN and ELVIS rush to her aid, they pick her up and sit her down.

---

* Guru Arjan, Guru Granth Sahib p. 1299

ELVIS: Better get her to the toilet.

ELVIS puts her in the chair.

BALBIR: No! I feel born again. Like I'm wearing a brand new nappy. I want to receive the Guru's wisdom and to sing the song of the holy word. I've found God Min. I've found him.

MIN: Flip!

BALBIR: I feel the need to worship, to make my peace... Will you take me inside?

MIN: Yes mother...yes...

ELVIS starts pushing the chair. BALBIR turns to face him.

BALBIR: Stop! You don't come Elvis darling...this is to be a private time for me and my girl.

MIN: Oh mother, thank you...thank you...

MIN goes to wheel BALBIR out.

ELVIS: Wait...you can't go off like this.

MIN: We won't be long.

ELVIS: Min, just give me a moment...

MIN: You've done more than enough already.

ELVIS: No...I haven't...

MIN: I don't know how I'll ever repay you.

BALBIR: We shall pray that your future is one of glory and prosperity.

ELVIS: Please don't go.

MIN and BALBIR head off. MIN beholds ELVIS with apologetic eyes.

MIN: Have a rest. You've earned it.

ELVIS watches them go.

Scene Seven
GURDWARA – A gentleman's agreement

MR SANDHU's turban is off and he plays darts as before. TEETEE stands close by him. MR SANDHU doesn't look at TEETEE. However she doesn't take her eyes off him.

SANDHU: Pala?

TEETEE: India.

SANDHU: He'll be back soon.

TEETEE: He won't be back. He doesn't want England any more. Or me.

SANDHU: These things pass.

TEETEE: He called me an ugly old cunt.

SANDHU: Words…mean nothing.

In the background MIN and BALBIR enter the worship area. They bow in front of the book and place coins down. They go to sit by POLLY.

TEETEE: I don't want him. I hope it's not long before he dies.

SANDHU: You shouldn't utter such phrases.

TEETEE: I try not to.

SANDHU: You have your boys.

TEETEE: Oh yes…them…

SANDHU: Be proud.

TEETEE braces herself.

Any sign of grandchildren?

TEETEE: Sunny's wife has left and Channa's isn't far behind. They are sometimes not very good boys. They like too much television and also quite young girls.

SANDHU: You should give them a chance.

TEETEE: Oh… I know it is not their fault.

SANDHU: Boys need chances.

TEETEE: And I am hopeful for Billoo…

SANDHU: The unmarried one?

TEETEE: Yes. The others have never suffered you see. Have never been hit or punched or anything. And now I have to suffer their lack of suffering. They are spoilt, and so they spoil everything they get their hands on. But Billoo was lucky, from an early age, when I saw my failures with the others, I would remember to kick him often and also pull his hair at regular intervals. We understand one another's many past afflictions and so you see he is the only person who loves me. Who I can rely on.

SANDHU: What on earth are you talking about?

TEETEE: He is setting up his building firm you know. And his aspirations…give me some hope.

SANDHU: What do you want Bhanji?

TEETEE: For Billoo…to build the extension to the Gurdwara.

SANDHU: That that…is a big task.

TEETEE: I will help him, don't you worry about that. (*A beat.*) You haven't made your decision yet have you Beerji?

SANDHU: Does he have access to all the necessary technical advisory people?

TEETEE: All of them. He has done labour and his friend is a plumber, another an electrician, one more a carpet fitter.

SANDHU: Can he understand an architect's plans?

TEETEE: Certainly. He communicates brilliantly with persons at all levels of society.

SANDHU: And he will give me a good price?

TEETEE: The cheapest gora cowboy cannot compete with my Billoo.

POLLY exits the worship area.

SANDHU: Why Bhanji do you want this?

TEETEE: He needs something. We need something. Of standing. For his future.

SANDHU: There is nothing else you can attempt?

TEETEE: No-one else I can ask.

She moves closer to SANDHU but looks away.

I will do anything Beerji, to help my boy.

SANDHU retreats from her.

SANDHU: I require only one thing.

TEETEE: Yes?

SANDHU: That I can count on you.

TEETEE's face almost crumbles, it's as if this is the worst thing MR SANDHU could have said to her.

I need people I can depend on.

TEETEE: I know.

SANDHU: So you are on my side?

TEETEE: (*A beat.*) Always.

Scene Eight
GURDWARA – Soft and lovely feelings

A toilet cubicle and a sink. ELVIS washes his hands. POLLY approaches but spots GIANI JASWANT coming out of the cubicle and quickly retreats. She moves out of his sight and hovers nearby. The GIANI sits down cross-legged next to the sink and starts clipping his toenails. ELVIS regards him anxiously.

ELVIS: Listen mate…are you sort of…a vicar?

The GIANI looks away, worried.

GIANI: I don't approve of labels or any kind of branding.

ELVIS: You help people though?

GIANI: (*Nervous.*) When you wish to perform a task, call upon God to assist.*

POLLY moves closer and listens in.

ELVIS: Are you confidential?

GIANI: I don't really like to know things.

ELVIS: Please…I have to talk. I need some advice.

GIANI: I've already told my story today.

ELVIS: It's important.

GIANI: And I ought to go and pray.

ELVIS: (*Urgent.*) What do you do if you like someone, and you wanna tell them, but if they don't like you back, you don't wanna make it all funny between you.

POLLY moves away out of earshot. She starts jumping around and throws her hands into the air joyfully.

Cos you have to keep seeing that person, twice a day and when you leave you're all soft and dreamy about it. About them.

* Granth Sahib, p.91

Excited POLLY turns back to eavesdrop.

You keep imagining what it'd be like, you know if you walked up the street together or got on a bus and sat next to each other or gave them a present or something. What I'm saying is…what do you do? For the best.

GIANI: I could…er…ask the one above…and see what he says…

ELVIS: There's not time. I've only got half a chance you see. She's probably already met some dreamboat with all prospects and stuff. Today. It's got to happen today. Cos tomorrow, everything's gonna be back like it always is.

POLLY moves out of earshot and delves into her bag. She excitedly sprays her body with Impulse. She checks her make up and starts to do her hair.

Do you know Min?

GIANI: My brother…knows people… I don't…

ELVIS: Her mum had that stroke.

GIANI shakes his head.

The dad topped himself ages ago. It was in the papers.

GIANI: I have always been in his shadow. A few steps behind. He is a more capable individual than myself, so perhaps you should turn to my brother.

ELVIS: (*Not listening.*) Min's the one. So good she is…so kind and pretty and decent. I mean I see her give Balbir a slap now and again, but only when she warrants it, which is most days if you ask me. After I've had a morning of cleaning and feeding, I go round and she's there all high and happy. She likes to move about and dance, oh you should see her. Wish I could be like that, she feels stuff, feels things proper deeply. And really she deserves a proper dreamboat. I know she does. (*A beat.*) But I love her. And I don't see how he could love her

like I do. I want to win her. And if I did, I'd save her. I'd
nail meself to a cross like Jesus Christ and let her be.
And if I could, just for one day, take her and bring her
places and show her new stuff and sit next to her. I
would. It would give me a point you see. I've not got
much point. That's my problem.

GIANI: Wonderful.

ELVIS: So what do you think?

GIANI: That is quite wonderful.

ELVIS: What do I do?

GIANI: You want to apply action to this problem?

ELVIS: Yes.

The GIANI springs up, perturbed.

GIANI: I am sorry. But I must go and change my
undergarments.

*The GIANI hurries out. ELVIS is flummoxed. An overjoyed
POLLY appears in front of him.*

ELVIS: Oh hello.

POLLY: Thank you Elvis.

ELVIS: For what?

POLLY: You sillybilly…

*ELVIS is about to say something but POLLY places a finger
on his lips.*

No more words…or questions or doubts or imaginings.
The answer to everything you are wondering…is yes.

ELVIS: Yes?

POLLY: Yes, yes, yes, yes, yes and a thousand yeses more.

ELVIS: I don't…

POLLY silences him again with her finger.

POLLY: When I was young…people used to say I was beautiful.

ELVIS: I heard…

POLLY: But I haven't felt beautiful, not for the longest time. You see so very deeply don't you? Inside people.

ELVIS: What?

POLLY: And you can see it in me now?

ELVIS: Oh…yeah…right…well you're lovely…of course you're ever so lovely.

POLLY: Really?

ELVIS: You are, honestly. Bet you were a proper stunner when…

POLLY moves towards ELVIS and kisses him on the lips. He responds and they embrace passionately. After a moment he hurriedly withdraws.

(*Mortified.*) I'm sorry… God… I'm so sorry…

POLLY: For what you silly?

She kisses him again and he responds. The GIANI comes back in. He stares at them. ELVIS notices him and recoils.

ELVIS: Oh God…

GIANI: I was under the impression this was the men's…

POLLY: Please Gianiji… I assure you…

ELVIS: I've never done this before. I swear I haven't…

GIANI: My toenail clippers…

POLLY: Things aren't what they seem.

GIANI: I don't want to see things…

ELVIS: Please don't tell anyone…

GIANI: But I keep being shown things….

POLLY: We were just discussing…er…perhaps you can help Gianiji.

POLLY hurriedly produces the paint pamphlet. The GIANI grabs his toenail clippers.

What is your favoured choice of colour for the new extension?

The GIANI hurries out. POLLY goes to take ELVIS' hand, but he moves away.

ELVIS: I've spoilt it all.

POLLY: Don't be perturbed.

ELVIS: I'm just a big load of nothing.

POLLY: Elvis!

ELVIS: Forgive me.

Dazed, ELVIS runs out.

Scene Nine
GURDWARA – Persuasion

MR SANDHU throws one last dart but doesn't bother retrieving it. Instead, with great gravitas, he puts his turban on and heads off in the opposite direction from the screen. Using her frame, BALBIR walks towards the screen. MIN has her arms around BALBIR and guides her gently. MIN looks around confused.

MIN: I think the girls' toilets are the other way.

BALBIR: I don't feel the need.

MIN: But it's time you went.

BALBIR: No. Coming here has given my bladder renewed strength and vigour.

BALBIR indicates the screen.

He's in there.

MIN pulls away from her mother.

MIN: No mother. I can't…

BALBIR: Please… Min…

MIN: I want us to worship.

BALBIR: But I've already said my piece.

MIN: Then let's do sayva.

BALBIR: I'm disabled.

MIN: You could hold a tea towel and dry some kitchen utensils. What kind of Sikh are you?

BALBIR: The same as all the others. What about you?

MIN: I'm trying to be…normal.

BALBIR: If you're not going in, how do you plan to pass your life?

MIN: With you.

BALBIR: And if I take a knife and slit my throat tomorrow?

MIN: Isn't it time to go home now?

BALBIR: No.

MIN: We've been outside long enough… I'm not really sure how to look at people or what to say any more…

BALBIR: Before your father went, there was an outside…

MIN: … And I don't feel very safe.

BALBIR: No need to be afraid Maninder…not here…

MIN: Elvis must be starving. He's too well mannered to help himself.

BALBIR: When I am gone…there will be no Elvis.

MIN: Don't say that.

BALBIR: Bloddy shitter! It will happen one day! You will have no-one. No father, no mother, no brother, no sister, no neighbour, no friend, no job, no place, no hope. The council will put you in a ticked box…you will have to pay for everything and if you are lucky you will go to work with angry people who laugh at you and steal your money and ping your bra strap.

MIN: (*Unsure.*) I'll be alright.

BALBIR: Your flesh came out of me, it is mine, my property. You are the only thing on this earth that remains of me, and I won't let those shitter social workers file you away.

MIN: They won't.

BALBIR: They already have… You'll never belong or fit or be anything, not on your own… Not with your father's blood in your veins…

MIN: He was sad.

BALBIR: Sad and useless. He is the reason I have to protect you and plan for you.

BALBIR puts her arms around her daughter, this is the first affection she's shown MIN in a long time. She hugs MIN warmly and then falls over.

MIN: (*Heartfelt.*) Mother…

MIN helps BALBIR up.

BALBIR: Forgive my…harshness?

MIN: Yes…

BALBIR: My beta, my darling, my baby girl, all I want is to take care of you…

MIN: Do you mean it?

BALBIR: I do.

MIN: You're not pretending?

BALBIR shakes her head.

BALBIR: Please…let me pay back some of the compassion and devotion you have shown me…

MIN's deeply touched.

MIN: Yes mother…thank you…sometimes I suppose I expect the worst.

BALBIR: Like your dad.

MIN: I don't want to be sad like my dad.

BALBIR: You won't be. Whatever those fat shitters think… I say you are a winner. And that you deserve a prize.

MIN: I always fancied an Olympic bronze. In gymnastics.

BALBIR: Yes.

MIN: Or showjumping even.

BALBIR: I have been reflecting for a very long time. And have concluded that this is the way. The only way forward. If you really want to get that medal.

MIN: I might.

BALBIR: And one day…you might find that you can become…something else…

MIN: Like the begaggled man…

BALBIR: A champion even.

MIN: Like a butterfly.

BALBIR: Yes, that's right. That's the spirit. Moreover there is a side of you, a feminine angle that it is time to explore.

MIN: Explore.

BALBIR: Feelings that you have never felt. Sensations you have never sensed.

MIN: Sometimes I think I may have feelings and sensations.

BALBIR: Good girl. Now all you have to do is have a natter with Mr Sandhu.

MIN: I'm not sure that's possible.

BALBIR: There is no time to wallow in the luxury of self-doubt. Think of all the others who will be affected by your sorry vacillation.

MIN: Others?

BALBIR: A Government compelled to pay you billions in social security, charity workers forced to call on you with dustbin bags full of used underwear and non-perishable goods. And my restless soul, tortured by the knowledge of your fleabag solitude.

MIN: Oh dear.

BALBIR: I expect God would want you to consider such others as well as other unmentioned others. To combat all that suffering.

MIN: I don't want anyone else to suffer. Because of me.

BALBIR: Go forth. Then and only then is there the chance that Things and You might have a different outcome.

MIN: Suppose I should forget about my feelings. For God's sake.

BALBIR: Yes. And I imagine that…God will be extremely pleased with you.

MIN: That's what I asked for…back there…

BALBIR: He'll be over the moon.

MIN: Will I be free then mother?

BALBIR: Free?

MIN: Of all that's criminal and…wrong about me…

BALBIR: Oh yes.

MIN: Does he remember me?

BALBIR: The years appear to have withered away his mental faculties.

MIN: (*Awkward.*) What's he like?

BALBIR: A gentle mouse, a widower whose wife's tragic departure was not unlike your father's.

MIN: I don't have to do anything… I mean I don't have to do anything today?

BALBIR: Just go and talk to him.

MIN: But can I? Do you really think I can do that?

BALBIR: I'm almost certain you can.

MIN: And whatever happens you'll be on my side.

BALBIR: Absolutely… Now Maninder… (*She points to the screen.*) In there.

MIN: You wait for me.

BALBIR: Where am I going, without my little girl?

MIN tentatively regards the screen. She slowly stands up.

MIN: Must be coming here today.

BALBIR: What?

MIN: Brought us closer together.

BALBIR: Yes.

MIN anxiously moves towards the screen.

MIN: Say a prayer for me mother.

Scene Ten
GURDWARA – True Colours

MR SANDHU walks towards the book. He kneels down, moves his head to the floor and then stands up. He puts his hands together and closes his eyes as though he is deep in prayer. He retreats slowly and sits down. He assumes a meditative pose and rocks gently to mesmerising Punjabi chanting.

ELVIS hovers by the stainless steel workstation. POLLY approaches cautiously.

POLLY: Do you want some rice pudding Elvis? It's extra milky Golden Temple style. Eat it and you will turn into a Jat Sikh farmer, big and strong, two metres tall and three metres wide.

ELVIS: No thanks.

POLLY: Why would you want to anyway? When you are perfect as you are.

ELVIS: About before… I didn't mean to offend you or anyone…

POLLY rushes towards him and takes his hands.

POLLY: Let's get out! Now!

ELVIS: I don't know what happened. I feel so bad.

POLLY: I have a jeep style vehicle in the car park, we can find a country road, recline the seats and let the love songs blare out loud and proud.

POLLY moves to kiss him again, and again he responds, but then draws away.

ELVIS: This isn't right…

POLLY: You have given me such hope.

ELVIS: I never meant to.

POLLY: Precious, wondrous hope. I am breathing and feeling and seeing and tasting like never before.

ELVIS: Tasting what?

POLLY: (*Laughs.*) You poor, strange, wild child!

ELVIS: That bloke's gonna tell on me…and it'll all be over before it's even started.

POLLY: Let him tell.

ELVIS: No!

POLLY: We'll live like outcasts and hold our heads up high and sell our story to the papers if there's enough interest. We'll shop together in anonymous supermarkets and scour holiday brochures for cottages in remote hilly locations. I'll wear micro-minis and drink babycham! We'll live like kings!

POLLY kisses him again but ELVIS quickly pushes her away.

ELVIS: (*Shouts.*) Get off me!

POLLY: Elvis?

ELVIS: I don't want that…

POLLY: But before…I felt…

ELVIS: I'm sorry…

POLLY: You said you liked me. That you wanted to walk up streets and get on a bus and give me a present. Why did you say all that?

ELVIS: It's not you.

POLLY: Then who?

Silence. The truth dawns on POLLY.

POLLY: I made you feel…sexy… I know I did.

ELVIS: I couldn't help it…

POLLY: You would choose a buffalo over me?

ELVIS: I don't know you.

POLLY: But I'm beautiful.

ELVIS: So's she.

POLLY: (*Vehement.*) No she isn't!

ELVIS: This is my fault. I shouldn't have…

POLLY: (*Hisses.*) No you shouldn't…you shouldn't love people and then take your love away just because there's a buffalo in the distance.

ELVIS: I didn't intend…

POLLY: To torment my soul?

ELVIS: Please…

POLLY: (*Upset.*) To hurt me? You think you can come in here and play with me as though I am an empty can of Fanta?

POLLY goes to attack ELVIS, however he manages to hold her at arm's length. She tries to hit him and they struggle. TEETEE enters.

TEETEE: Bhanji?

ELVIS lets go of POLLY, she stumbles but manages to hold herself up.

ELVIS: I'd better go and find Balbir.

POLLY: Teeteeji…this boy…

ELVIS: I have to fill out a sheet you see. Otherwise there'll be trouble.

POLLY: He is not what he seems.

TEETEE moves in front of ELVIS blocking his way.

TEETEE: What has happened?

ELVIS: There's been a misunderstanding.

POLLY: He…he…insulted me…

ELVIS: No…look… I'm trying to do my job.

TEETEE: You don't come in here and insult the ladies of the Gurdwara.

ELVIS: I never.

TEETEE: That is for the ladies to do.

POLLY: Gianiji witnessed the incident.

TEETEE: That is extremely serious cause for concern.

POLLY: And (*Points.*) he and the buffalo girl are up to something.

TEETEE: I might have known… Did he insult you…badly?

POLLY: Yes, oh yes…but…I managed to…protect my honour.

TEETEE: What shall we do?

POLLY: Tell him off Bhanji, you tell him off good and proper!

TEETEE takes ELVIS' face harshly in her hand.

TEETEE: No rules in here boy. No police, no laws, no evidence, no witnesses, no nothing.

ELVIS: You threatening me?

TEETEE laughs, she lets go of him but stares at him intently.

TEETEE: Remember one thing boy. There is a man's soul in this woman's body. Our men are cruel to our women but we get used to it and we follow the rules, letting each slap and tickle and bruise and headbutt go by. And at the end of this rubbish life, we write the rules. We find the beauty in our cruelty. My daughter-in-laws suffer just as I suffered. I make sure of it. Things happen. And no-one can do nothing. Because everything must stay the same.

ELVIS: I don't know what you're on about.

POLLY: Tell him Bhanji!

TEETEE: You be careful boy.

He goes to head out. TEETEE stops him in his tracks with a traditional Sikh salutation.

Vaheguruji kha khalsa …

ELVIS is stuck, he doesn't know how to respond.

POLLY: (*Furious.*) … Vaheguruji khi fateh.

ELVIS pushes past TEETEE and heads out.
BALBIR watches MR SANDHU walk out of the worship area.
Agitated ELVIS walks into the GIANI.

ELVIS: Please don't say anything. To Min.

GIANI: I don't like to speak, but people keep asking me things.

ELVIS: I don't want her to know me like this. I couldn't stand it.

GIANI: Before the bedraggled man entered the front room… He was like you…he was experiencing feelings like you. And that was I think, is possibly…when God was truly happiest.

ELVIS: (*Breathless.*) I'm juss dreamin' and imaginin' and pretendin'… Who am I? I can't do nothing apart from bring her up the pub…

GIANI: I have therefore concluded…that you must tell the person in question.

ELVIS: Tell her?

GIANI: (*Chants.*) Jo bole so nihal: Sat Sri Akal.

ELVIS shakes his head, perplexed.

He who says this is saved: Truth is the immortal Lord.

Sikh religious music plays. The GIANI holds his hands together and walks towards the worship area. He bows respectfully to the holy book and then goes to sit behind it. TEETEE and POLLY also advance and kneel down before the book. GIANI JASWANT soberly waves the stick of horse-hair. TEETEE and POLLY sit cross-legged with their heads covered on the women's side. TEETEE turns to POLLY, they speak in loud whispers.

TEETEE: Who made the parshad?

POLLY: Fatty Grewal.

TEETEE: He always overdoses the ghee. You have mine.

POLLY: (*Dejected.*) I can't eat… Put it in a tissue and flush it down the toilet.

ELVIS leads BALBIR in.

ELVIS: (*Anxious.*) Where's Min?

ELVIS helps BALBIR Muthateck (pray respectfully in front of the book), he does the same and then walks her over to the women's side.

BALBIR: Leave her alone.

ELVIS: You better tell me.

BALBIR: What are you going to do? Wipe my arse to death?

ELVIS: I'll find her.

ELVIS turns to go, BALBIR clutches onto his arm for dear life.

BALBIR: You are supposed to look after me.

ELVIS: I am.

BALBIR: What about your sheet? If you go, I won't sign it. I won't sign. (*A beat.*) I'll say you went off and left me and it'll be true. They won't let you come round any more, they'll send someone else.

ELVIS is torn.

(*Gentle.*) Don't say nothing, not yet…wait…just wait…

BALBIR is now seated. TEETEE and POLLY regard ELVIS disdainfully. He stands desperately on the ladies' side.

(*Hissing at ELVIS.*) You are causing the embarrassment!

ELVIS uneasily goes to sit on the men's side. BALBIR turns to the ladies.

He is not my usual staff.

GIANI JASWANT starts a religious chant in Punjabi.

GIANI: (*Translation.*)
God always looks after the weak, protects believers and destroys evil
Birds, beasts, snakes, mountains and kings;
God cares for all forever
Sees all beings in the sea and on land
Does not dwell on their past sinful deeds
Benevolent to the poor, an ocean of compassion
Watches sinners but does not stop bestowing gifts on them.*

Scene Eleven
GURDWARA – Gulthee
(Mistake/Wrongdoing)

MIN is alone in Sandhu's office area. She paces around, not knowing what to do. She examines the Sikh paraphernalia and picks up the

* Guru Gobind Singh, Dasam Granth, Swayyai

kirpan. She starts having a swordfight with an imaginary opponent. She moves around vigorously and becomes increasingly relaxed. On the desk she notices a BeeGees CD and regards it, surprised. She hums 'How Deep is your Love' and sways while still holding onto the kirpan. As the musical feelings rise inside her, she starts to dance with the kirpan, her movements are big and bold and fill the space. While she is humming and dancing, MR SANDHU enters. He watches MIN. Suddenly she spots him, and stops dead. They contemplate each other.

MIN: I'm…

SANDHU: I know.

She hands him the kirpan. He puts it back in its place.

You looked like you were enjoying yourself.

MIN: I didn't mean to…enjoy myself.

SANDHU: How are you?

MIN: I don't know.

SANDHU: We met when you were little. In the park. You were riding a purple tomahawk.

MIN: Did you have a greasy face?

SANDHU: No…I'm sure I was well groomed.

MIN: I don't remember much.

MIN shuffles around awkwardly.

SANDHU: Please sit.

MIN: What…me?

SANDHU nods. MIN obediently goes to sit behind the desk. Awkward silence. MIN indicates the CD.

What you doing with music?

SANDHU: It keeps me… (*Thinks for a second.*) …going.

MIN: I know what you mean.

SANDHU: Through all the bad moments…and believe me there've been enough of those. You know…sometimes…

MR SANDHU breaks down.

I find it all very hard…

Concerned MIN watches him cry like a baby.

No-one understands my plight.

MIN: Don't depress yourself.

MIN reaches in her pocket and takes out a scrunched up tissue.

Here you are…

SANDHU: Thank you. Thank you very much. For being so caring.

MIN: It's only been used once.

SANDHU: Guilt is a very difficult feeling to bear.

MIN: I know.

SANDHU: Yes I suppose you do. How on earth…is one supposed to cope?

MIN: Put a smile on God's face, and he'll forgive us all our sins.

MR SANDHU composes himself.

Are you better now?

SANDHU: Much better. Yes. Much better. (*A beat.*) I…er…understand you are looking for someone.

MIN: Sort of.

SANDHU: What kind of individual?

MIN: Any.

SANDHU: And what kind of person are you?

MIN thinks on this.

MIN: Female.

SANDHU: You have a beautiful name.

MIN: I always wanted to be called Sally.

SANDHU: I expect you want to see the list?

MIN: I don't…not really.

SANDHU: Then why are you here?

MIN: My mum told me to come.

SANDHU: I see.

Silence.

MIN: Can I go now?

SANDHU: If you like.

MIN: I don't want to miss the paug.

MIN gets up to leave.

SANDHU: Tej would have been proud of you.

MIN stops.

MIN: I haven't done anything.

SANDHU: You seem to follow your own mind.

MIN: Do I?

SANDHU: Just like your dad. He…also followed his heart.
    Do you do that?

MIN: I couldn't say.

SANDHU: Is there anyone…inside your heart?

MIN: Sometimes…I think so.

SANDHU: His name?

MIN: Secret.

SANDHU: What does it begin with?

MIN: E…

SANDHU: Next letter?

MIN: That's enough…

She heads out.

SANDHU: You know, your father was extremely melancholic.

MIN turns to face him.

MIN: Did you help him put my stabilizers on?

SANDHU: Yes I did, he and I…we used to go on long walks.

MIN: While I went round and round.

In the worship area, the congregation stands and chant the last Aardas – traditional Sikh song at the end of the reading of the Granth Sahib.

SANDHU: You know when we came to this country, we were all so hopeful. Not that things would be much better but that they wouldn't be any worse. And that they might be different. We wanted possibilities and options, to wear ties and frequent pubs. And to feel carpet underneath our feet. I wanted to be a man, not a son or a brother or a husband.

MIN: (*Confused.*) You…you are…

SANDHU: You buy and sell and eat and excrete and inhale and exhale and do all the things you said and that you wanted. And all that happens is that you end up. You just end up.

MIN: End up what?

SANDHU: Tej knew.

MIN: I don't understand all this.

SANDHU: I'm a very selfish person.

MIN: (*Encouraging.*) Bet you're not.

SANDHU: Whatever things look like, there is always another story, always the truth underneath the show. After a while we get used to the disappointment. We don't even have to live with it because we pass our failures onto our children. Like you. And then everything becomes your problem.

MIN: Shall I go now?

SANDHU: I have failed.

MIN: You haven't. You've got a desk and a chair.

Smiling, MIN regards the religious paraphernalia.

And loads of other bits and pieces. (*Pointing to the kirpan.*) Look.

SANDHU: You must have heard about my wife.

MIN shakes her head.

I can see the blame and the pity in your eyes.

MIN: Who is she?

SANDHU: But you see I am so lonely, so very damn well lonely.

MIN: You want to get a telly.

SANDHU: So good. You are so so good. I can see it. I can see Tej in you.

MIN: My dad was sad.

SANDHU: I need someone you see.

MIN: Is she gone...your wife?

SANDHU: Yes. Thank you for realising.

MIN: Do you want to marry my mum?

SANDHU: You remind me of him...you remind me of my Tej...he...he used to kiss me...on the lips...hard...so fucking hard...

MIN: (*Disturbed.*) What?

SANDHU: You remember don't you?

MIN: No...

SANDHU: But you saw us...together...

MIN's getting distressed.

MIN: Please stop...

SANDHU: I wasn't to blame. You watched didn't you? When you were going round and round. Your eyes met mine. And his.

MIN: No.

SANDHU: He felt sick with himself for what you'd seen.

MIN: I didn't want to see. I didn't mean to.

MIN's sobbing.

SANDHU: Then he got on that train.

MIN: I know... I'm all criminal...

SANDHU: If you hadn't been there, he'd still be here. With me.

MIN: Please don't tell my mum.

SANDHU: There have been many lovers in my life...but none like my Tej... I loved him so fucking much... If only I could feel him...possess him... Just one more time… You've never been touched have you…there's been no physical contact…

MIN: Stop talking…please…

She turns to exit. MR SANDHU follows her.

SANDHU: He was a fine man, such a nice person. Good to be around and spend time with…like you.

Before MIN can head out. MR SANDHU grabs her. She struggles.

MIN: Get off me…get off…please get off…

Her screams and shouts merge with the end of the Aardas (song) in the worship area.

Scene Twelve
GURDWARA – My flesh and your blood

Sikh religious music plays. GIANI JASWANT distributes parshad. He first goes to ELVIS, who eats it, then to POLLY and TEETEE who surreptitiously stuff it in tissues and put it in their handbags, and finally to BALBIR who solemnly eats it. ELVIS helps BALBIR up. TEETEE and POLLY head out. BALBIR shakes ELVIS off and, using her frame, follows the ladies. ELVIS comes forward and approaches the shoe rack. He looks around. The music fades. ELVIS calls out.

ELVIS: I'm waiting for you Min… I'll call you, I know if I call, you'll come to me.

He starts to sing 'You are the Sunshine of my Life' with simple, beautiful clarity.
A blank-faced MIN appears. She hobbles along slowly and sits down on a small stool a distance away from ELVIS. She listens to ELVIS singing.
He looks up and meets MIN's eyes. He stops singing.

Don't say anything. Please. I just want you to hear.

ELVIS gathers all of his courage together.

Coming here. It's been like you said. All special. Proper special. I'm starting to feel like you feel. You know when you dance an' that. Like I can do deeds and speak words I couldn't before. I feel…brave. Like I'm someone who sings all the time. (*A beat.*) You've moved me Min… Maninder, you've made me feel like I'm flesh and blood and bone and hair. And…and…I love you… I've loved you from the first moment I saw you. I know that I'm a right waste of space but I want you to know that… I'd be honoured to have you on my arm. (*A beat.*) If that's at all possible. Ever. (*A beat.*) What d'you think?

MIN: Where's my mum Elvis?

ELVIS: She went off with them ladies. Kitchen I think.

MIN: Thank you. (*She gets up.*) You go home. I'll manage now.

ELVIS: What about what I said?

MIN: I don't know.

ELVIS: Doesn't it matter?

MIN: No.

ELVIS: Did that vicar bloke warn you…about me?

MIN shakes her head.

Then they must have got you a dreamboat. Someone with qualifications and transport. Good-looking. Bet he smells nice and does exercise… But you know…you won't ever be to him, like you are to me.

MIN: There's no-one.

ELVIS: Please let me take you out. Once?

MIN shakes her head.

You never go out.

MIN: I can see out on the telly.

She heads off, ELVIS stops her.

ELVIS: She…she hasn't signed my sheet.

He produces a piece of paper from his pocket. MIN blankly takes it.

MIN: You'll have to wait…

ELVIS: You're being…different.

MIN: Stop talking.

ELVIS thinks for a moment.

ELVIS: (*Sings.*) Precious Lord, take my hand, lead me on, let me stand…

MIN: (*Shouting.*) Shush up! You're home care, you're not supposed to sing.

ELVIS: I didn't mean to offend you. I would never be like that to you, and if you don't like me any more…can't say I blame you…

MIN: I have to…go to the girls' toilets. Then I have to see my mum.

ELVIS: I'll walk with you.

MIN: No.

ELVIS: Why?

MIN: Private.

ELVIS: Say…please! I…know you don't I?

MIN: How dare you! How dare you presume anything about me!

ELVIS: I'm not…

MIN: (*Slowly to herself.*) She probably got called away. She'll be waiting somewhere, wanting to give me another cuddle…

ELVIS: Min…

MIN: (*Shouts.*) You have no right to address me. You're not even anything to do with me, you're here for her and look…you're prancing around, in this religious area, saying things. Things that don't concern me. You're flipping well home care, right, and that's it! Get out of my way.

ELVIS stays put.

(*Shouts.*) Please Elvis!

After a moment flabbergasted ELVIS shuffles forward so he has his back to her.

Don't move from here…promise me you won't move…

He nods.

Stay…and you'll get your sheet signed.

MIN hobbles off. As she walks, we see a terrifying patch of blood staining the back of her clothes.

Scene Thirteen
GURDWARA – Behzti (Dishonour)

Standing at the workstation, TEETEE and POLLY mechanically wash and wipe kitchen utensils. BALBIR sits nearby, drying stainless steel beakers with a tea towel. POLLY appears flat and distracted and TEETEE's mood is downbeat. BALBIR however is almost unable to contain her excitement.

BALBIR: The deed is surely done by now. And I will be calling upon my dear friends for assistance.

POLLY: Assistance?

BALBIR: Men with glittery turbans must be recruited to make merriment, horses and carriages need to be booked and the cheapest food is to be purchased in the largest quantities. Ladies, our daughter, Maninder is to be wed.

113

POLLY: The buffalo girl?

BALBIR: Mr Sandhu has chosen her.

POLLY: Her?

BALBIR: To be conjugated with a name on his list.

The GIANI enters.

TEETEE: His famous list…

The GIANI picks up a handful of pakoras and stuffs them in his mouth. POLLY hurries over to him with a stainless steel thali, which he accepts.

POLLY: How are you Gianiji?

GIANI: *Comme ci, comme ça.*

TEETEE: I understand that earlier you witnessed an insulting happening.

POLLY: We ought not to dwell on that event Teeteeji.

BALBIR: What occurred?

TEETEE: Elvis Singh was misbehaving himself.

BALBIR: You must understand he has a brain disorder. Pity the boy.

POLLY: Best forget it, isn't that right Gianiji?

GIANI: I try my best to forget everything but pictures stay in my head, even when I ask them to leave.

POLLY: I hope…that…all is not lost for the wretched individual…

GIANI: Sadly we are all lost.

POLLY: Everyone is permitted to make one mistake, surely?

GIANI: My brother says it only takes one tiny morsel of excrement to attract a hundred flies.

POLLY: Better if we do not ever talk of this again.

GIANI: (*Sad.*) If I am spoken to, I speak back… I am afraid I have never been much good at exercising control.

He exits. POLLY's face falls.

POLLY: You should not have brought that boy here Bhanji.

BALBIR: Can I count on you dear friends?

TEETEE: I hope you are planning a function with all the relevant traditions in place. Without our deep and meaningful customs, the event will be false and flimsy.

BALBIR: I would rather my ears were gnawed off by starving rodents, than risk such desecration.

TEETEE: You have settled her fate then Bhanji.

BALBIR: Oh yes.

TEETEE: And you are willing to pay the price?

BALBIR: I can contribute a modest three figure sum, left by the deceased for this exact purpose. I imagine any further extravagance will be taken care of by whichever capable person emerges from the list.

POLLY: You can't tell people the groom is from a list. It's embarrassing. Shameful.

TEETEE: Best keep your trap shut about that one.

POLLY: They will want to know there has been an introduction…

TEETEE: By the bacholan…

POLLY: So it's safe… I mean we can't have just anyone betrothed to whatsherface.

TEETEE: And the bacholan will have traditional requirements.

POLLY: Gold earrings. Twenty four carat.

TEETEE: A diamond for the nose is essential.

BALBIR: You will have everything you want…

POLLY: Us?

BALBIR: But I must be able to rely upon your help, your guidance…

TEETEE: Who else is there Bhanji?

BALBIR claps her hands and punches the air with glee.

BALBIR: It will be like the old days.

POLLY: The good old days.

TEETEE: Choosing shinky shonky material, with a foil takeaway tub of chaat in one hand…

POLLY: Buying new tupperware…

BALBIR: Sitting in a circle, applying mehndi, singing the old bollees.

TEETEE claps to the gidha beat.

TEETEE: Sus meeri thi jumia billa.
Oh mahnji ah kee gilla gilla?
(My mother-in-law gave birth to a kitten.
Ooh missus, what's that wet thing between your legs?)

The women laugh. Suddenly MIN enters.

Here comes the bride.

MIN: Mother…

BALBIR: Not now ducks, we're talking about you, not to you!

She chuckles. MIN approaches BALBIR.

MIN: Please mother…

TEETEE and POLLY notice MIN's bloodstained shalwar.

I don't quite know how to speak this…

POLLY: Cursed girls and ladies do not come to God's house at that time of the month!

MR SANDHU approaches from the distance, but remains unseen by MIN and BALBIR.

BALBIR: For shitter's sake…stupid girl!

MR SANDHU makes sure that POLLY and TEETEE see him.

POLLY: You should not have brought this disrespectful buffalo here Bhanji.

TEETEE: Is it your intention to insult God?

POLLY: So much behzti. Nasty filthy dog!

TEETEE: Maybe it is up to us to teach her Pollyji. For all our sakes.

MIN: But it's not my time.

TEETEE and POLLY drag MIN over so that she has her back to BALBIR, they show her mother the stain.

POLLY: Look at your dishonourable daughter Bhanji.

TEETEE: Importing her dirty monthly blood into the Gurdwara.

MR SANDHU discreetly exits. The ladies hold MIN firmly by each arm as if she is a criminal.

MIN: I haven't. Honest to God I haven't…

POLLY: Liar, liar pants on fire.

BALBIR: There must be some explanation…perhaps she has the excitement because of the wedding…

MIN: There's something mother…I have to say. Privately.

BALBIR: A bride has no secrets from her bacholan.

MIN: What?

BALBIR: My friends are also your mothers.

TEETEE: There are no excuses for this unwelcome patch of red.

MIN breaks away from the ladies, she's in a state of acute distress.

MIN: Please. I don't know what to do.

TEETEE: You are all muddled up.

MIN: No… I'm not…

TEETEE and POLLY move towards MIN.

BALBIR: Keep your eyes on the medal Maninder. That bronze disc you so merit.

POLLY: Shut up Bhanji. You leave this to us.

MIN moves away from the ladies.

MIN: Stay away from me, you…cows.

BALBIR: Maninder!

POLLY: Such filth is coming out of her mouth.

BALBIR: Do not be hard on her…please…she does not understand the ways of usual people.

TEETEE: Then it is our duty to explain…what is required of her under this roof.

The ladies move closer to MIN. Frightened, she turns away from them but they carry on a menacing advance towards her. Suddenly she makes a run for it, but POLLY swiftly grabs her. They tussle.

BALBIR: Min…we must realise…it is occasionally necessary to follow a series of twisty side roads before one gets onto the motorway.

*TEETEE joins POLLY and they start to beat and kick MIN.
She cries out in pain. TEETEE drags her over to BALBIR
who is close to tears.*

TEETEE: Your turn Bhanji…

BALBIR: It may appear harsh, but there are some ways of
the world that you and I have to understand…

BALBIR weakly slaps MIN round the face.

To adhere to…

She slaps her again.

To get used to…

*There are shouts of 'Gundhee kuthi' (dirty bitch) and
'Behsharam' (shameless) from the ladies as they continue to
beat MIN up. MR SANDHU enters. TEETEE takes off her
chooni (scarf) and gags MIN with it.*

SANDHU: Stop this at once!

TEETEE and POLLY turn to face MR SANDHU.

We are not animals. Please try and maintain some level
of decorum.

*MIN remains on the floor, gagged, in a heap. MR SANDHU
beholds her sadly.*

All individuals make unforced errors.

BALBIR: Poor child, she has never recovered from the
behzti of her father.

TEETEE: Must have inherited it.

POLLY: And you with your toilet trouble. None of it helps.

BALBIR: It doesn't.

SANDHU: I have a suggestion that may put a silver lining
on this cloudy business.

MR SANDHU whispers in BALBIR's ear. TEETEE and POLLY bring MIN over to BALBIR and MR SANDHU. MIN stands before them as though she is a pupil who has been sent to see the headmaster.

BALBIR: Dear Maninder, there is something…there is the chance that something useful can emerge…

MIN shakes her head vigorously.

All of a sudden my bladder feels full to the brim.

POLLY takes BALBIR's arm.

POLLY: Beerji, I fear her mummy's presence is fuelling her insolent manner.

SANDHU: Thank you for your kindness Polly Bhanji.

MIN makes desperate noises. POLLY leads BALBIR out. MIN's getting increasingly upset. TEETEE unties the chooni.

MIN: (*Screams.*) I want my mother!

TEETEE: First you have to apologise to Mr Sandhu.

MIN points at MR SANDHU.

MIN: He put himself inside me (*Indicates her vagina.*) here…and he felt me…

TEETEE: You are expected to say sorry.

MIN: He knows what he did to me. And so do you. And so does God. And you can break every bone in my body and defile me further and bury me here and we'll all still know. Because that's what happened. That's the truth.

TEETEE: (*Shouts.*) Just say it!

MR SANDHU starts to cry.

SANDHU: What is a man to do? Then again she cannot help being a temptress. Perhaps I am at fault for being so easily enticed.

MIN attempts to run out, but TEETEE restrains her. There is a struggle which eventually TEETEE wins. She holds MIN around her neck. She drags her back to face MR SANDHU.

TEETEE: Say sorry you buffalo!

MIN: I won't.

TEETEE: Do it!

MIN: Never. I never will.

TEETEE: Does Balbir Bhanji like pain?

MIN: No…you cow…no!

TEETEE: Does she like to be hit and punched and scratched and all her clothes taken off?

TEETEE pulls her hair hard. MIN starts to cry.

One little word.

MIN is in agony.

My sons will fuck her up the arse till she bleeds a river of blood.

MIN sobs.

Hurry up.

MIN: (*Whispers.*) Sorry…

TEETEE releases MIN, she falls over in front of the desk. TEETEE goes over to SANDHU. Tearful and emotional, she spits on his feet.

TEETEE: She's yours.

TEETEE exits.

SANDHU: Are you hurt?

No response. MIN stares at the floor.

The first time there is bound to be some pain. It will get better.

Silence.

You remind me of him so much. I was unable to help myself. I adore you, you see. Just as I loved your father. So damn madly. He was always scared of our passion. Embarrassed. And that's why he went the way he did. He broke my heart. But now he has come back to me, through you. (*A beat.*) Would you like a sweetie?

MIN shakes her head.

Have this then.

He takes the BeeGees CD out of his pocket and hands it to her.

There is something I must ask you.

MIN looks up.

I just mentioned to your mother…I was wondering if…if…you would like to marry me? When we are husband and wife there will be no need for all this.

Long silence.

MIN: (*Slowly.*) You lied.

SANDHU: Why don't you take some time to think about it?

SANDHU goes to exit.

MIN: You've done this before haven't you?

SANDHU: Yes…yes I have.

MR SANDHU exits. MIN beholds the CD. She attempts to hum 'Emotions' but cannot. The only noise that comes out of her mouth is atonal and off key. She tries to move about, but her stiff, tired body won't go anywhere or do anything. Exhausted, MIN slumps onto the floor. TEETEE comes back in.

TEETEE: (*Gruff.*) Sometimes buffalo girl, you have to make a sacrifice. For the good of everyone, you realise?

No response.

You want some tea?

No response.

Sweet milky tea helps.

TEETEE goes to get the tea. BALBIR enters and approaches MIN.

BALBIR: Did he pop the question?

MIN nods.

And you are alright?

No response.

Was there something you wanted to tell me?

MIN: There's nothing.

BALBIR: Speak for shitter's sake.

MIN: Doesn't matter any more.

BALBIR: So you are happy to marry him?

No response. TEETEE comes back with a cup of tea for MIN.

I want you to be happy. Besides, he hasn't got much longer on this earth. You'll end up with the sort of bank balance that will attract a fine young specimen.

TEETEE eyes BALBIR coldly.

TEETEE: Quiet now Bhanji.

MIN: You have to sign Elvis' sheet mother.

BALBIR: I forgot about that shitter.

MIN takes the sheet out of her pocket. She struggles over to BALBIR and gives her the sheet, which BALBIR duly signs.

Yes, we will be alright now. Everything will be alright. You go and get things ready Maninder. I'll wait here.

MIN goes to exit. TEETEE holds out the cup of tea to her.

TEETEE: It's finished.

No response.

You'll be going home soon.

TEETEE reaches out to MIN. But MIN strikes her arm and the tea goes flying. MIN exits.

BALBIR: Forgive her, she has been a boil waiting to erupt.

TEETEE: She's braver than she looks.

BALBIR: Funny how things turn out. I for one was set on the list…but such things do not allow for plain old-fashioned attraction. I didn't know she had it in her…but perhaps she's more of a chip off the old block than I gave her credit for. Don't be perturbed by her demeanour. She's shocked I know, she's come over all strange…all because she can't believe her own bloddy bollocks. She came looking for a fish and caught a bloddy whale. Perhaps I'll be the one asking my son-in-law for his list.

TEETEE: (*Flat.*) There is no list.

BALBIR: What?

TEETEE: No fucking list.

BALBIR: (*Shocked.*) Bhanji?

TEETEE: You stupid old cow.

BALBIR: Of course there is a list. Mr Sandhu told me…he talked to me…

TEETEE: Did he ever show it to you?

BALBIR: No.

TEETEE: Did you ever ask to see it?

BALBIR shakes her head.

BALBIR: You're being silly.

TEETEE: It doesn't exist.

BALBIR: You're lying… Teetee?

No response. BALBIR's getting more agitated.

Why would he say there was one when there wasn't? What reason?

TEETEE: Why do you think?

BALBIR is paralysed with shock.

So that girls go up and see him. So he can force them… And boys sometimes. He likes to rape people.

BALBIR: No he wouldn't…he would never do that…you said he is a gentleman…

TEETEE: I didn't.

BALBIR: You know he is…we all know him…

TEETEE: He did it to your girl.

BALBIR: You bloddy liar. He loves Min and she will grow to love him. They fancy each other.

TEETEE: (*Screams.*) Is that what you think of your daughter you sick bitch?

BALBIR: Why are you doing this Teetee? Why are you saying such evilness?

TEETEE: It's true.

BALBIR: How do you know?

TEETEE: (*Flat.*) Because he did it to me.

BALBIR takes this in.

Right over there.

TEETEE points to a corner.

125

BALBIR: No…no…this is not…is not feasible…you are trying to trick me and confuse me…

TEETEE isn't listening. She points again. She speaks in a matter of fact fashion.

TEETEE: They stripped me first and covered my mouth. Then he bent me over and pulled my hair. He was young then so he had better control. Your Mr Sandhu went inside me and took what was human out of my body. My mother wept salty tears while she watched. Afterwards she beat me till I could not feel my arms or legs. Then she turned to me and said, now you are a woman, a lady. Now you are on your own, behsharam.

BALBIR: I told her to go in because he said there was a list.

TEETEE: They must have left you out Bhanji.

BALBIR: So you…you stood by…while I sent my Min…

TEETEE: Yes…

BALBIR: But you…you beat her…you said she was at fault…

TEETEE: I do my duty.

BALBIR: You made me hit her.

TEETEE: You did that yourself.

BALBIR lunges at TEETEE. She misses her pathetically and lands on the floor.

BALBIR: (*Fearful.*) It couldn't happen…not before my eyes…like this…

TEETEE: It just did.

BALBIR: You let it…you made it…

TEETEE: I tried to warn you Bhanji.

BALBIR: You made me…

TEETEE: That's what passes.

BALBIR becomes breathless, it's as if she is having a panic attack.

I am sorry you were not aware.

TEETEE gets up to exit. Distressed BALBIR shouts after her.

BALBIR: Where are you going?

TEETEE: Home. In a little while.

BALBIR: (*Screams vehemently.*) This business isn't finished. You don't do that to my girl…and just go home…you don't…you can't…

TEETEE stands at the exit. BALBIR crumbles.

(*Despairing.*) What will happen to her now?

TEETEE: (*Cold.*) Same as the rest of us…

TEETEE exits. BALBIR breaks down. She cries out through her tears.

BALBIR: No. Never…never!

BALBIR sobs her heart out.

Scene Fourteen
GURDWARA – Izzat (Honour)

MR SANDHU is at his desk flicking through the paint pamphlet. POLLY and the GIANI sit in front of him.

SANDHU: Sunwashed stone.

POLLY: I was thinking…possibly…double cream.

SANDHU: Possibly double cream.

POLLY: With a russet leaf ceiling?

SANDHU: Interesting.

GIANI: I like lilac.

SANDHU: What did you say?

GIANI: It is a contemplative colour.

SANDHU: No. Not that.

POLLY: No.

SANDHU: Beige perhaps.

GIANI: I…I find lilac flowers appealing.

SANDHU: Have you been seeing lilac flowers?

GIANI: Occasionally.

SANDHU: And other things?

POLLY: So we're agreed on sunwashed stone. Or double cream.

MR SANDHU gets up and stands over the GIANI.

SANDHU: Tell me what things.

GIANI: Please… I really would like lilac to be considered.

SANDHU: Jaswant, have you been sourcing Class A substances?

GIANI: Not since the bedraggled man was in the front room…

SANDHU: (*Interrupts.*) Tell the truth.

GIANI: I am. Meditation and meditative colours help people…

SANDHU: Have you been displaying inappropriate behaviour?

GIANI: …to feel happy feelings and…escape their demons.

SANDHU: (*Shouts.*) Have you?

No response.

Say thank you.

GIANI: Thank you.

SANDHU: For rescuing me from my demons.

GIANI: For rescuing me from…the one who made my heart beat.

SANDHU: Jaswant!

GIANI: I adored her.

SANDHU: Shut up!

GIANI: I think of her most days. I pray for us…even though I am undeserving of God's care.

SANDHU: She went to prison…to pay for your sins.

GIANI: I am in prison. I beg him to save me.

SANDHU: I saved you.

GIANI: To spare me from the hell in my heart.

SANDHU: From her. I protected you from the filth inside your bones. Say thank you.

GIANI: Thanks.

SANDHU: What did you see?

GIANI: A…lady…

SANDHU: What must one do with the demons one sees?

GIANI: Give them away.

POLLY: The extension Beerji!

SANDHU: What was the lady doing?

GIANI: Snogging…a black boy.

SANDHU: Where is she?

The GIANI gets up slowly.

GIANI: It is a modern, multicultural colour.

After a moment, he points at POLLY. He is on the verge of breaking down.

POLLY: No Gianiji! No!

GIANI: I am very fond of it.

He exits.

POLLY: If there is a tone we particularly like, I can enter through the trades entrance, perhaps there I might find an exact match.

SANDHU: There is to be an immediate review of the distribution of tasks in the Gurdwara. You will be taking no further part in our plans for the extension.

POLLY: Will I still be able to get the shopping in?

SANDHU: No.

POLLY: What…what will I do then?

SANDHU: That is for God and the committee to decide.

Teetee enters, MR SANDHU nods at her, acknowledging her presence. POLLY looks away.

(*To POLLY.*) But for now...

MR SANDHU hands POLLY a notepad and pen. He paces about.

In your best handwriting. (*Dictates.*) Dear Gerry, I am writing to verify receipt of the council's correspondence regarding the planned extension of the Westbury Road Sikh Temple. In brackets Gurdwara.

POLLY writes this all down.

I, Mr R S Sandhu, as the spokesperson for our committee, am grateful for the very good points you have made regarding our application. We await, expectantly, the expansion of our religious home, a further indication that we form an integral part of our town's thriving coffee-coloured melting pot. And I am more than happy to provide you with the information you requested.

MR SANDHU looks straight at TEETEE.

I can confirm that Mr B D Thompson will be charged with the responsibility of carrying out the building works.

TEETEE absorbs this. She almost crumbles.

Mr Thompson has had a long and prosperous business relationship with the committee of the Sikh Temple. In brackets Gurdwara. It could be said that he is regarded by many, as one of us, and we, as one of him. With regard to your other very good points, I would like to point out, since its arrival spanning the last forty years, the Sikh community has played an important role in the development and flourishing of our town. Our principles of hard work, humility, family values, coupled with our integrationalist attitude…in brackets, for example going down the pub…have stood us in good stead…

TEETEE: (*Interrupts.*) Pollyji… You said I could have a lift.

POLLY doesn't move.

I didn't know you did…shorthand.

POLLY: I'm doing my best to learn.

SANDHU: (*To POLLY.*) My throat is feeling rather dry… I wonder if…I might have a very large cup of chah.

POLLY gets up.

It would be nice if you could also locate some gulabjaman.

POLLY walks out. MR SANDHU and TEETEE eye each other.

TEETEE: Found a new lackey?

SANDHU: One always comes along. Isn't it Teetee?

TEETEE: And my son?

SANDHU: There will be some other role for your boy.

TEETEE: I explained…this was all I wanted. One little thing…

SANDHU: The future of the Gurdwara is not a little matter…

TEETEE: That you give him one small chance…in return all you have taken…in return for stealing my body and my soul…

SANDHU: I have taken nothing that was not being readily given.

TEETEE: You have left me with nothing.

SANDHU: This is not a job for Indians…sometimes we have to defer to the greater authority of our white brothers…

TEETEE: (*Shouts.*) You promised!

SANDHU: I really am very sorry…

TEETEE: I will tell the police. I will tell everyone the truth about you.

SANDHU: Who will believe you Teetee?

TEETEE: You try and stop me!

SANDHU: Witnesses watched as you beat that unfortunate girl. Black and blue. Only when I intervened did you stop. I really ought to have you ejected from the building.

TEETEE lunges forward and pushes him over. He falls onto his desk. TEETEE grabs the kirpan and holds it over him. He whimpers fearfully.

TEETEE: Bastard…

SANDHU: I try to be good. I did try…

TEETEE: Why does God make us live amongst such bastards?

SANDHU: Forgive me…

TEETEE: In the seventeenth century…

SANDHU: Forgive my sins…

TEETEE: (*Breathes deeply.*) …the Emperor Aurang Zeb ordered that all Sikhs be forcibly converted to Islam…his troops used to take our girls and impregnate them in order to taint their blood and defile the genes of their offspring… Guru Gobind Singh commanded his followers to fight, so that the souls of the Sikhs were preserved… Even when Aurang Zeb's soldiers buried his sons in walls their resolve would not weaken… But afterwards he proclaimed it was time for the raising of swords…there were also the blessed Gurus before, martyrs who sat on hot plates and defied death… And now our glorious mantle is passed on to preserved souls…like you…

BALBIR hobbles in.

SANDHU: Please…

BALBIR: Stop!

BALBIR approaches.

Teetee…you can't…

Shaken, TEETEE lowers her arm.

Wait…just wait…

BALBIR approaches TEETEE and takes the kirpan out of her hand. Lights fade.

Scene Fifteen
GURDWARA – Resurrection

MIN stumbles towards ELVIS.

MIN: She's signed it…

> *MIN's badly hurt and almost out of it, she hands ELVIS his sheet.*

ELVIS: Min…

> *MIN falls into his arms.*

What's happened?

MIN: I…had an accident…

> *She just about manages to stand. ELVIS holds her tightly.*

ELVIS: Okay…it's okay…

MIN: Take me to a tap… I need a wash.

> *Stunned, ELVIS carries her into the men's toilets where GIANI JASWANT is splashing his face in the sink.*

ELVIS: Excuse me…vicar…sir… I need some help…

GIANI: I have already helped you. Or not?

MIN: I'm alright…

> *MIN gets to her feet. ELVIS shows her into the cubicle.*

ELVIS: You…you go and sort yourself out, I'll be here…

> *ELVIS closes the door on the cubicle. He approaches GIANI JASWANT.*

(*Frustrated.*) What you doing just standing there? Something's happened.

GIANI: Those who beat you with fists, do not give them blows…

ELVIS: I can't hear this any more…

GIANI: Go to their homes yourself and kiss their feet.*

ELVIS grabs the GIANI and shakes him.

ELVIS: Stop now alright. Stop!

GIANI: I saw you…kissing… I saw…

ELVIS: I don't care.

GIANI: The bedraggled man felt love…before…he felt
what you feel… God knows…

ELVIS: What are you on about?

GIANI: If only I could serve him adequately. But I
cannot… I am unable… I beg you…kill me…please kill
me…

ELVIS: Shut up! Shut up!

He shakes the GIANI again, and his turban falls off.

GIANI: You live… I want my life to end. Live…please…

ELVIS goes for the GIANI again. MIN emerges.

MIN: Leave him Elvis!

*ELVIS lets the GIANI go, he falls to the floor. MIN addresses
the GIANI.*

I only came here to say happy birthday and I didn't even
manage that. I wish I had sung it then, because right now
I don't know about praising. All you lot in here…
perhaps you talk too much…best sometimes to keep
things inside…why do you always have to Say…and
Show and Make it known what you are? How good you
are…how kind and nice…rich and beautiful and
worthy… Cos what if you're not perfect and what if it all
goes horribly wrong and there's no sign of coloured
wings flying in the sky? Then what do you do and where

* GGS p.1378

135

do you go? Seems to me like everyone's pretending the same as each other. Just letting the outside sparkle and twinkle like flipping well fairy lights. I had hopes. They weren't anything special. But they were there. Now I'm beginning to get why people walk around like they do with sallow skin and blinking eyes, not ever really looking at each other, because they can't face…they can't face…the sight. And my praising, it's nothing to do with this… You know… I'm ever so glad I'm not you lot… cos it must be difficult, all that pretending all the time… Next time…if I still manage to praise… I'll tell him about you lot, perhaps he'll help. See if he can…yes… If I can…I'll ask him…for all of us…

She moves closer to the GIANI and speaks gently.

Vaheguruji kha khalsa… Vaheguruji kha khalsa…

The GIANI shakes his head, unable to respond, he remains huddled in a corner. ELVIS approaches MIN.

ELVIS: Tell me.

MIN: No…no…

ELVIS: I'll help you…

MIN: What's it got to do with you? You can't take over my things.

ELVIS: I wanna look after you.

MIN: I look after. I take care. I do all that. For nothing. I'm not home care, I'm just a person. And if I can do it for her, I'll do it for myself. (*A beat.*) Anyway it's finished now.

ELVIS: You know… I love you Min…even if you don't love me…

MIN: (*A beat.*) Oh but I do. I do…with all my heart I do…

ELVIS: Are you sure?

MIN: I must. I can feel it now, more than ever. But you see I don't know what it means because the truth… sometimes…it lets you down Elvis.

ELVIS takes her hand. They don't let go of each other but stand apart.

ELVIS: Let's get out.

MIN: Can't just leave her.

ELVIS: Come with me…

MIN: No.

ELVIS: Why?

MIN: I don't know. Cos I'm hers. Cos she's all I've got.

ELVIS: There's me now. We're together.

MIN pulls away from ELVIS.

MIN: Whatever's happened…I'm still that thing I was before…that's all I am…

ELVIS: You're more now.

MIN: I don't know all your stuff. Like where you live and where everything goes and what the mornings are like and what colours are about…

ELVIS: You'll learn… I'll teach you…about life…

MIN: Learning's not for stupids like me.

ELVIS: You ain't givin' yourself a chance.

MIN: Do you know when my birthday was?

ELVIS shakes his head.

Or what my best telly programme is?

ELVIS: Don't matter.

MIN: Or what I do when she's in bed or when she's eating?

ELVIS: You dance.

MIN: Not any more. And I'm violent. Sometimes. Often.

ELVIS: I love you.

MIN: It's not enough Elvis. Not for old stupids. I'm sorry.

ELVIS: (*Ferocious.*) I'm not having that. I'm not having it.

ELVIS grasps her hand.

I'll help you. And I'll look after you. And her if I have to. We'll hold hands and wheel her about and we won't care about anything that isn't to do with us.

He holds her to him. He starts dancing with her around the space. At first she moves awkwardly.

And I want to see you dance.

She loosens up.

And dance.

They're flowing now.

And dance till you drop dead.

MIN laughs despite herself. She's half crying, half laughing. She starts to dance by herself.

MIN: Look at me Elvis. Look at me!

ELVIS: You're beautiful.

MIN moves elegantly around the space.

See…you're free again.

MIN: Perhaps I am. I feel I am. Like it's all begun from now.

ELVIS: That's right.

MIN: This second.

ELVIS pulls MIN towards him. They hold each other tight. Suddenly there is the sound of stainless steel falling to the floor nearby, followed by a deafening scream. ELVIS runs off in the direction of the scream but is hurriedly halted by TEETEE. A dazed BALBIR approaches MIN.

TEETEE: (*To ELVIS.*) Take them home.

The scream turns into a wailing chant of 'Satnam, satnam, satnamji, Vaheguru, vaheguru, vaheguruji' which continues over the following action.

I will do my duty.

BALBIR shows MIN her hands, they are stained with blood. They whisper to each other. Their words are almost inaudible.

BALBIR: Vaheguruji kha khalsa…

MIN: Vaheguruji khi fateh.

Trembling BALBIR goes to hold MIN's face in her hands. They behold each other for a few moments. Then MIN draws away from her mother. MIN turns away and stretches out her arm to touch ELVIS. Fade to Black.

THE END

Glossary

bacholan: matchmaker

beerji: brother

behsharam: shameless

bollees: village chants

bucharah: poor thing

chappals: sandals

Ek Umkar, Satnam: One God, named truth

goreh / gora: white

kauthi: big house

kheer: rice pudding

meh tha Darghi: you scared me

mehndi: henna

methi dhi roti: fenugreek bread

parshad: religious food

Sat siri akal: Truth is the immortal Lord

thali: plate

Vaheguruji kha khalsa: God be with you, the members of the Khalsa belong to God

Vaheguruji khi fateh: All victories are God's